PASSIC

Discourses on Blackwomen's Creativity

Edited by Maud Sulter

Maud Sulter was born in Glasgow, Scotland in 1960. She has a Masters degree in Photographic Studies and writes and lectures extensively on Art History, specialising in Women's Art practice 1840-1990.

Active in debate around cultural politics since 1982, Ms. Sulter holds the MoMart fellowship, as Artist In Residence, at the Tate Gallery Liverpool, 1990-1991.

Ingrid Pollard was born in Guyana and came to Britain as a child. She holds a BA in Film Studies and continues to document photographically Blackpeople's creativity and presence in the diaspora. Her work has been exhibited in many galleries in Britain and the USA.

Maud Sulter is the author of *As A Blackwoman*, Akira Press 1985: UFP 1989 and *Zabat: Poetics of a Family Tree*, UFP 1989. She is currently registering for a PhD under the supervision of Professor Griselda Pollock at Leeds University.

AN URBAN FOX PRESS CULTURAL STUDIES IMPRINT

British Library Cataloguing in Publication Data
Passion: Discourses on Blackwomen's Creativity.
    1. Arts. Black women. Creativity
    I. Sulter, Maud, *1960-*
    701.15

    ISBN 1-872124-30-5 (hbk)
    ISBN 1-872124-31-3 (pbk)

UFP, PO Box 2, Hebden Bridge, West Yorkshire HX7
Printed at the Arc & Throstle Press, Todmorden, Lancs.
Typeset by Bridge Business Services, Hebden Bridge, West Yorkshire.

Contents

SECTION FOUR
TESTIMONY   229

Illustrations

Preface

It is time now
to let you go
a book can fly on its own wings
and I therefore
shall practice mine

It is a luxury uncommon to most Blackwomen to have just one job and run a home. During the decade it has taken to bring this collection to book several of the contributors have worked two, three, even four, jobs; most lowly paid, in underfunded projects, shops, factories, offices and domestic settings. Then, of course, there has been political activity: on the street campaigns, behind closed doors campaigns and the every day tenacity of making something creative of family life.

Living in the aftermath of slavery and enforced migration the very notion of Black family life comes under constant external pressure. Section 28, anti-homosexual legislation, the erosion of the Welfare State in the UK, rising homelessness, immigration controls and current attempts to legislate against the autonomy of single mothers all mitigate against home life.

While working and homekeeping we also seem to have endeavoured to gain access to education and qualifications – which are not necessarily the same thing, as many in this collection observe.

That said we have witnessed a decade of change in the creation of Blackwomen's creativity to which this book bears testimony. There are no martyrs in our struggle but there are women who have fallen and we each remember our own friends, colleagues, lovers, and even adversaries, too many of whom have been debilitated by bodily sickness, mental weariness and domestic/state violence.

This book has changed form (and title!) on at least three occasions, usually spurred on by the promise of a feminist publishers contract being 'in the post'. I no longer apologise to myself for my naïvety, for without hope there can be no redemption for feminism. 'In the post' it transpires is a euphemism for another 18 month-2 year delay. The carrot being dangled – usually the promise of funds to complete the research, colour plates, launches, eternity even. However, none of their promises came to anything. Which is a tragic indictment of an industry that has become rich and powerful from the sales of Blackwomen's writings, that of Alice Walker and Maya Angelou in particular. This preface could be a litany of complaint, so much is unfair, unjust, unspeakable – however we must

9

keep *ourselves* centre stage, primary, at the core.

This collection situates itself primarily within an urban experience of Britain but takes an international perspective in recognising global struggles and the role of our creativity in helping to secure our economic, social and emotional liberation. The objective of this book is to offer a variety of perspectives of what it means to call oneself a Blackwoman artist. The endeavours and successes of Blackwomen's creativity are often criticised but seldom critiqued in a constructive upwards and outwards way. This leads to a fear of discourse and dialogue which undermines our aims and must be countered. Discourse is a primary tool against the weapons used to marginalise and write out of history our contribution *she who writes herstory rewrites history.*

We must break the cycle of reinventing the wheel. Every year young women write to me asking to interview me for their dissertations. After one particularly 'busy' spring I decided that I had better get myself a qualification so many BAs and MAs had I contributed to, which is how come a poor little coloured girl from the Gorbals who dropped out a long time ago and kept on dropping out comes to have five 'O' levels and a Masters Degree. So in one hour or occasionally one day's teaching in a college, art school or similar, one is asked to redress mis-education, mis-information and mis-direction.

It is painful to see the ignorance of which exhibitions, publications, meetings etc. have happened. Painful to recognise the fact that so much remains unread and unlooked at. More painful the seemingly perverse pleasure taken in the suicidal belief that one is the *only* one, the *first* one, *the* one.

There are many whom should and must be thanked. Ingrid Pollard for documenting so many important events and happenings, the contributors of such magical words and pictures, our multiple audiences who over the years have witnessed and taken the trouble to engage with what our voices have tried to say, and, of course, I wish to recognise the vision, wisdom and absolute passion for Blackwomen's Creativity of Lubaina Himid. Without who's endeavours there would be no *Passion: Discourses on Blackwomen's Creativity.* To her, our finest artist, this book is dedicated in the spirit of MaShulan.

Maud Sulter,
1990

Acknowledgements

The Publishers would like to acknowledge partial financial support from the Arts Council of Great Britain, Greater London Arts, The Women's Solidarity Fund, and the tremendous amount of unpaid labour by Blackwomen themselves without which this publication would not have been possible.

In particular we wish to thank Maud Sulter for her dedication and determination which she undoubtably underestimates! She has triumphed in spite of the trials and tribulations of funders, difficulties in gaining the confidence of her contributors that what they had to say was important and helping them realise their ideas on paper and has been brave enough to compile this collection in the face of a hostile society that daily tries to marginalise Blackwomen's Creativity.

THIS IMPRINT IN MEMORY OF

BEULAH MAE DONALD

PASSION:
Discourses on Blackwomen's Creativity

Maud Sulter

Introduction

As editor of this volume I am delighted to introduce its contents as a mere overview of the many creative Blackwomen working both in Britain and those in other locations who choose to work in collaboration with us.

The main body of the text is split into four sections:

1. A brief overview of The Blackwomen's Creativity Project, followed by a photo-essay by Ingrid Pollard which was selected from her vast and tremendously informative archive.

2. A stunning collection of new writings cover a spectrum of forms. Essays, poetry, and a speech. Some are accompanied by images. All address vital issues with regards to the politics of creativity and representation.

    This is the first UK collection in book form to articulate the hopes, fears and aspirations of Blackwomen artists and writers as activists and creative women. The Blackwomen's Creativity Project recognises a spectrum of creativity as art and literature; the criteria which makes it art is its application in the pursuit of carrying on the timeless tradition of Blackwomen's endeavour to create a more meaningful and better quality of life using myriad forms of artistic production in the pursuit of an aesthetic of informed pleasure.

    These qualities are often applied to political struggles as our experience of the new Europe (which has a suspicious odour of the old Europe) and American Imperialism leads us to confront racism and sexism. The power that maintains its position as creativity is the rigour with which the participants work to move beyond simple rhetoric to pure rhetoric – an agent of revolutionary change.

3.   The Portfolio section offers a selection of artists and their work in a variety of media: photography, printmaking, paint, clay. The majority of these women have participated in Blackwomen's Creativity Project and Elbow Room events.

4.   The final section is a collection of archive materials which give only a hint of the range of activities which have occurred over the past decade and signify a continuity for the future success of The Blackwomen's Creativity Project into the '90s and beyond.

There are many books which need to be written, *Passion: Discourses on Blackwomen's Creativity* should be read as a signpost to further research. It does not endeavour to document or index any more than those places where The Blackwomen's Creativity Project has touched fragments of the enormous web of activity.

To be a success this book should encourage all Blackspinsters out there not only to promote this publication but also to research, reclaim and make public our herstory for ourselves.

Take care of your blessings,
Maud Sulter, 1990.

Blackwomen's Creativity Project: an Overview

The Blackwomen's Creativity Project celebrates its 8th birthday with the publication of *Passion: Discourses on Blackwomen's Creativity*. In 1982 I was the first Black collective member of Sheba Feminist Publishers. It began as a knee-jerk response to a suggestion that the Collective should put together an anthology of Blackwomen's writing. I believed at that time, and I still do, that anthologies have the dangerous appearance of a Press having published a lot of Blackwomen writers. Anthologies need a lot of time and skilful editorial work to be a success for both the writer and the reader. It is a glowing testament to those Blackwomen who came after me at Sheba that they put together *A Dangerous Knowing: Four Blackwomen Poets*, and *Charting the Journey*.

I felt that it was important to open up other areas of Blackwomen's Creativity to the book form and took it upon myself to create just such a book.

I am not sure that I had ever knowingly seen a painting by a Blackwoman Artist (and I certainly did not know then that I myself would someday become just that, a Blackwoman artist!). But I knew that if writers existed then artists did too, so all I had to do was take the trouble to find them.

A short report back on a Black Arts Convention in Wolverhampton written by Ingrid Pollard and published in *Outwrite* led me to calling the author, alterting her to my idea and arranging to meet and discuss.

Ingrid shared with me the information she had and also invited me to **Black Woman Time Now** at Battersea Arts Centre in 1983. That exhibition had been curated by Lubaina Himid.

Together, Ingrid Pollard and I, began to work – she took pictures, I wrote words. Some of these collaborations appeared in publications such as *Artrage, Spare Rib* and *FAN* (Feminist Art News).

Our travels took us around Britain visiting cities such as Cardiff, Bristol and Belfast. We made the political decision to include Belfast as we knew that, contrary to what many people tried to tell us, Blackwomen lived there and if my theory about the tenacity of Blackwomen's Creativity was true then it would exist even in such a volatile and occupied location.

After leaving Sheba I took the Project into the Women's Education Resource Centre, which was looking for another project to complement Claudia da Silva's tremendously important Women's Self-Defence Project. During the first two years I spent there I not only encouraged the publication of more Blackwriting and images in *GEN* the Centre's anti-sexist anti-racist journal but also launched *Check It!*

Check It! was a celebration which ran at the Drill Hall for the month of July in 1985.

Week one opened with the launch of Claudette Johnson's *Images of Blackwomen* which was followed by *Blackwomen Writers Reading*. Amryl Johnson read from *Long Road to Nowhere*, Barbara Burford read *Miss Jessie* from *Everyday Matters* and some poetry including *Christine* which was later published in *Dangerous Knowing*.

A busy bar buzzed with excitement and the second half opened with Maud Sulter reading from *Tiger Eye* a short story and *As A Blackwoman* (Akira Press). Munirah brought the evening to a close by performing an exerpt from *On The Inside*.

The Young Women MCs Night included Lorna Gee, Sista Culcha and Cookie Crew. Yvonne Field from ILEA and Evelyn Marius from Women in Music Promotions judged an open-floor competition and the sparce but rowdy crowd enjoyed every minute. The event was a landmark in the development of rappers, breakdancers and MCs.

The next night saw the Asian Women's Writers Group read publicly for the first time. Kumari Nalini and her sisters danced and Terri NaaKoshie Quaye presented The Sounds of Africa – a recital of Ashanti Drums, Balofon and Sansa. Friday and Saturday night saw Elizabeth Sinclair and Lola Young in performance, and Meera Syal in *One of Us*. Mumtaz Karimjee's *Women in China* exhibition opened on the 16th.

The second week of events opened with a *Solidarity Evening with the People of Azania and Namibia*. Marsha Prescod read poetry from *Land of Rope and Tory* (Akira Press), Sistahs in Song appeared under that name for the first time, (later Voices for Oya), Lioness Chant caused consternation with an anti-lesbian poem, and Pamela Maragh-Lofton held the audience breathless with her stunning solo dance piece. She has since continued to dance and is now choreographer to Soul II Soul.

16

The FILM AND VIDEO event saw the launch of Claudia da Silva's *Women's Self-Defence* video. Later four films were screened in the theatre:

Reassemblage:	Trinh T. Minh-Ha
Illusions:	Julie Dash
Hairpiece:	Ayoka Chenzira
I Be Done Been Was Is:	Debra J. Robinson

The festival closed with two musical events. The penultimate night featured Sista Culcha and Shikisha. And on the final night Sista Culcha was once again at the controls, Lynda Murray and Friends played jazz, Gail Ann Dorsey sang accompanied by her guitar and Shades of Love brought the house down with their soul stirring gospel music.

It is interesting to look back at the statement printed on the brochure promoting *Check It!*

How come? As a blackwoman creativity is central to my existance. It is a means of survival, covering a spectrum as diverse as singing, sculpture, hairbraiding and childbearing our Art demands participation. Developing our skills, acquiring the means e.g. film equipment, paint, a piece of paper and a pen, and getting on and doing it is central to our success. In presenting images of ourselves we affirm our worth. Within a hostile urban environment we deconstruct dynamics of sex, race and class to survive.

From SULA by TONI MORRISON
"In her way, her strangeness, her naivete, her craving for the other half of her equation was the consequence of an idle imagination. Had she paints, or clay, or knew the discipline of the dance, or strings; had she anything to engage her tremendous curiosity and her gift for metaphor, she might have exchanged the restlessness and preoccupation with whim for an activity that provides her with all she yearned for. And like any artist with no art form, she became dangerous." (Published in the UK by Triad Granada)

Thanks to the support of the Drill Hall Arts Centre (yet another organisation threatened with closure when the GLC is abolished) over these two weeks thousands of people will bear witness to the quality, diversity and commitment of blackwomen's creativity. Some will be surprised, all will be strengthened.

Most importantly we will see that it can be done. Even with no funding, no advances, no outside support. What it takes is nerve. And I (who wouldn't say boo to a goose) for one didn't know I had it in me. Three years ago when I started work on *Check it!* the book (sounds like a movie!) all I had was a cheque book which was to write many a dodgy cheque and a belief that Art is not genetic. Contrary of course to the Western definition, made by white privileged males who are more renowned for their destructive qualities than creativity. Given the resources anyone can do it. But there are, as Toni Morrison points out above, dangers.

With the support of a wonderful photographer called Ingrid Pollard I travelled Britain finding women working in our Arts fields. We knew they were out there. Others wouldn't believe it. Witness me on the phone to the Scottish Arts Council (they presuming me white coz of the Scottish accent) "No sorry dear we couldn't offer funding or support for this project. There are no black artists in Scotland!"

These two weeks of events will open the floodgates of Blackwomen's Creativity in Britain. An area central to contemporary cultural production. Check it and support us next year with our planned international Black-women's Events.

Maud Sulter, Blackwomen's Creativity Project.

From that point the Blackwomen's Creativity Project has worked both independently and in collaboration to stage events such as *Testimony: Three Blackwomen Photographers*, Pavilion Gallery Leeds (1986), and shall continue to do so. Blackwomen's Creativity Project promoting Black-women's Creativity.

Blackwomen's Creativity Project IV

Ingrid Pollard

Photographs

Ingrid Pollard is a documentary photographer who has published her photographs in several magazines and journals such as *Spare Rib, Outwrite* and *The Voice*. She has exhibited prints widely in exhibitions in Britain and the USA. The first public viewing of her work took place at *Black Woman Time Now*, Battersea Arts Centre London, 1983 and she went on to show in *The Thin Black Line*, ICA London, 1985 and various exhibitions including: *D-Max* and *The Cost of the English Landscape*.

She has been documenting events and individuals for BWCP since 1983.

The photographs pictured here are only a brief selection from her extensive archive. They give an overview of the broad spectrum of Blackwomen's Creativity which she has documented in her own inimitable style.

She returned to education as a mature student and received a BA in Film Studies from the London College of Printing. Meanwhile she keeps up her photography and is a part-time teacher in further education.

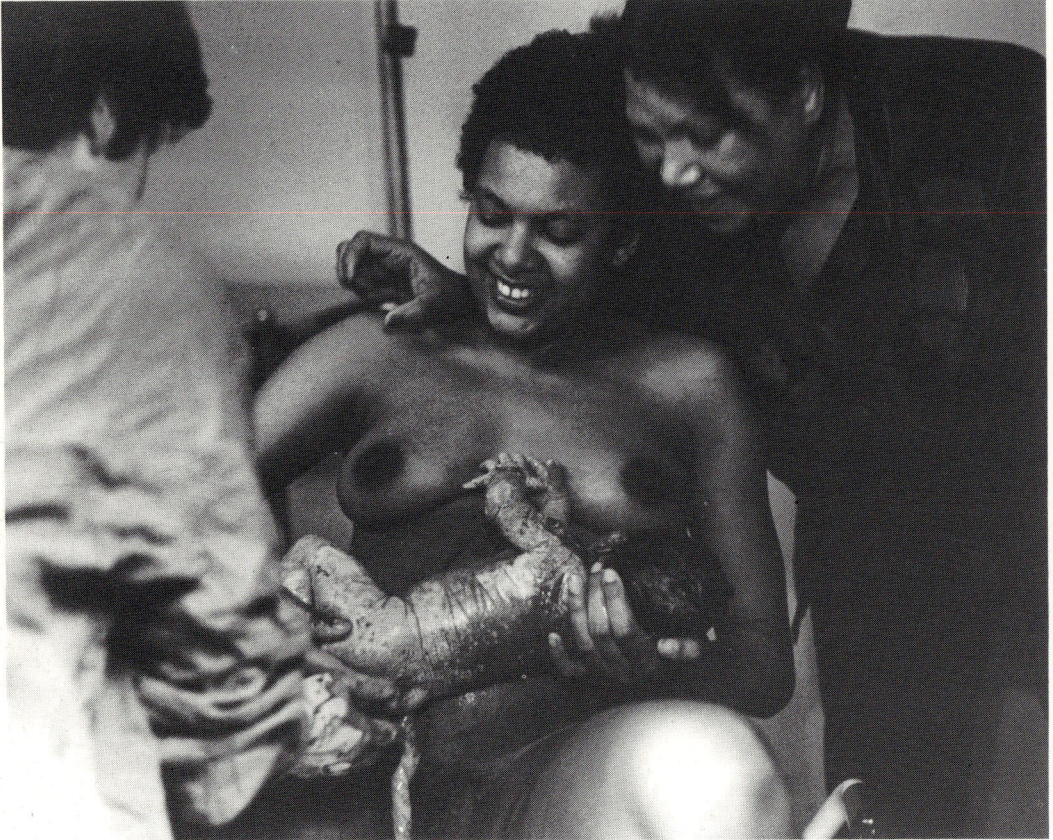

MARLA BISHOP, with mother, midwife and child

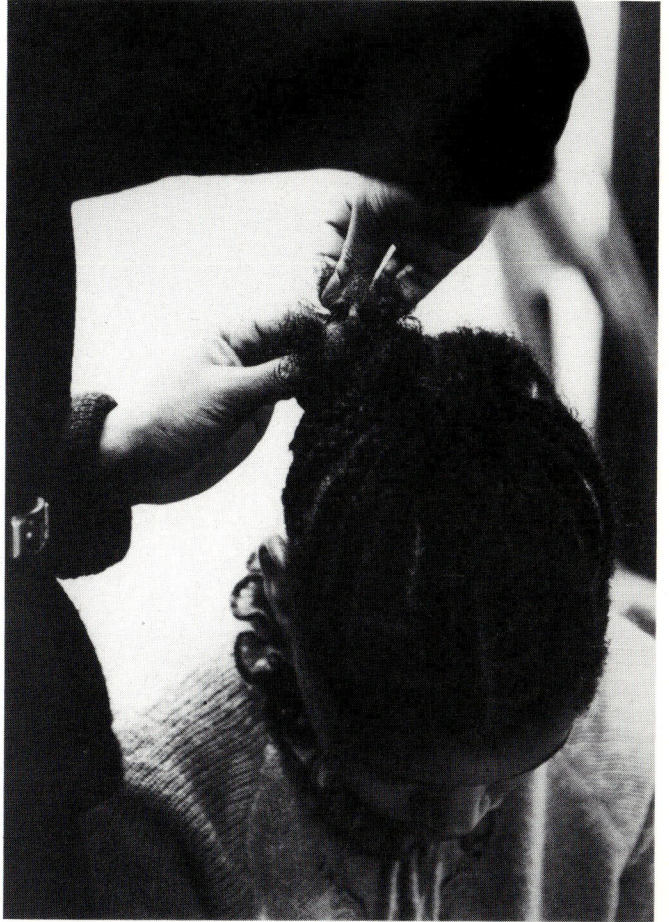

YEMI MORGAN, Hairbraiding

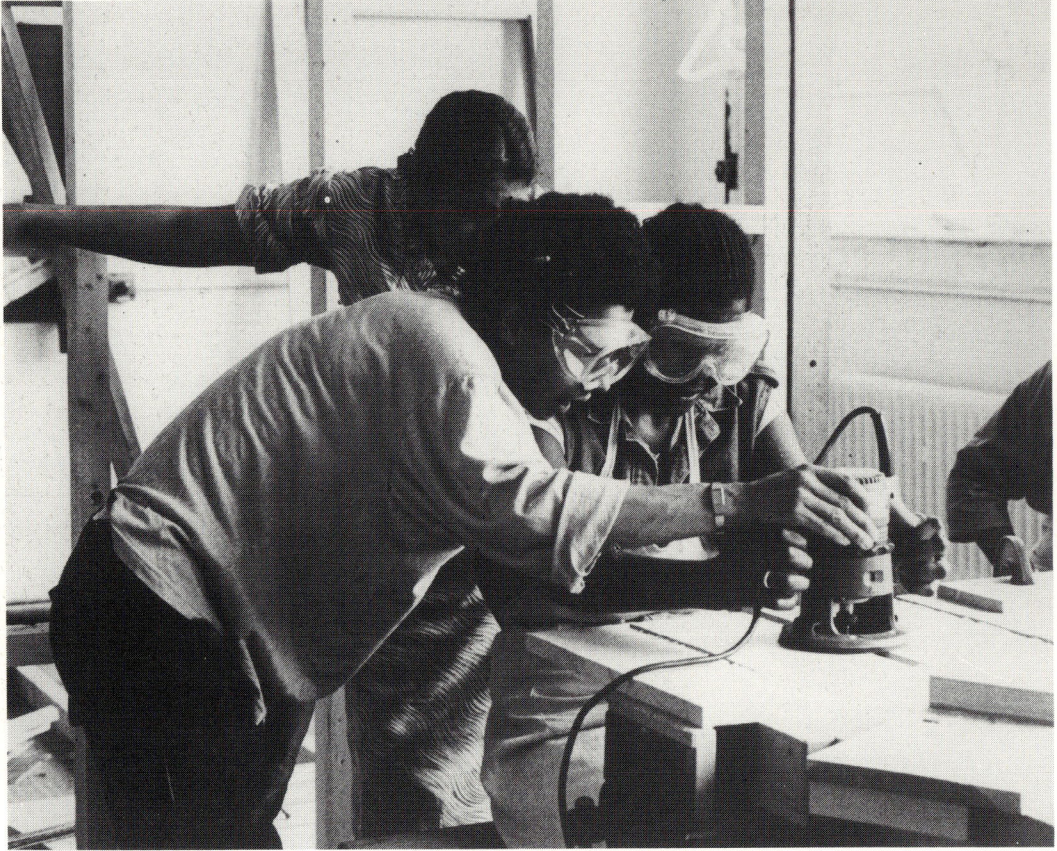

Blackwomen in Manual Trades

Black Pensioners' Group, Photography Workshop

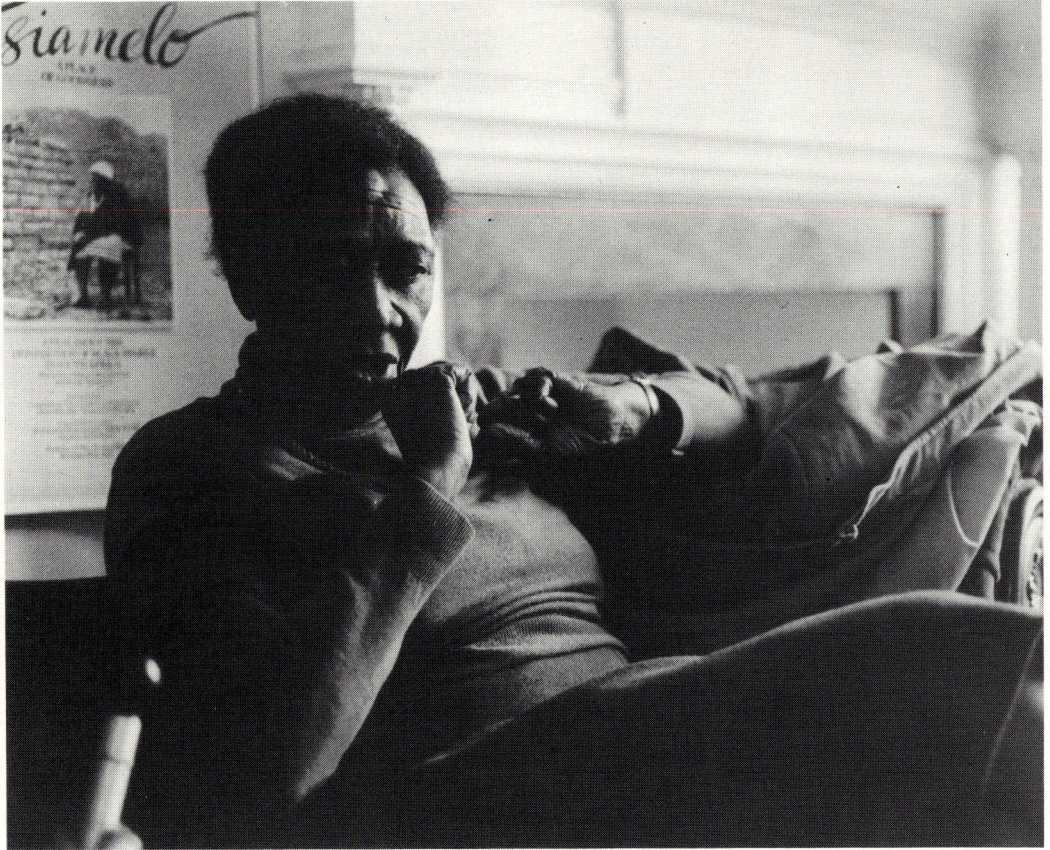

ELLEN KUZWAYO, writer and community activist from Soweto

MAYA ANGELOU, writer

MAUD SULTER, writer at *Sphinx,* an event organised by Talawa
Blackwomen's Group at The Pavilion, Leeds

Blackwomen editors, Feminist Bookfair, London 1984

JACKIE KAY, writer

SUNITI NAMJOSHI, writer

AUDRE LORDE, writer

GLORIA JOSEPH, writer

DOROTHEA SMARTT, writer and performer

SISTAHS IN SONG (renamed as Voices for Oya) presently
regrouping

THEATRE OF BLACKWOMEN

MUNIRAH, workshopping with children

THEATRE OF BLACKWOMEN and MUNIRAH, workshopping
together with SISTREN from Jamaica

MEERA SYAL, actress

NOTTING HILL CARNIVAL

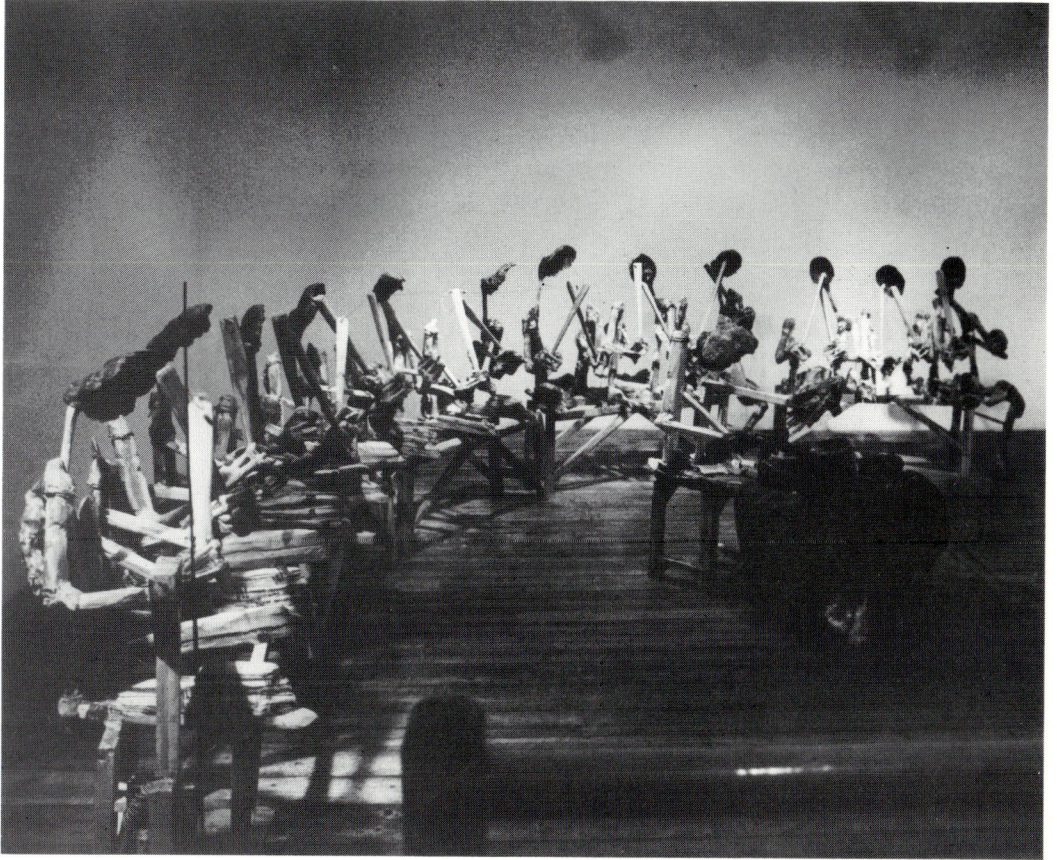

SOKARI DOUGLAS-CAMP, Sculpture

CHILA BURMAN, printmaker

NINA EDGE, Ceramicist

MAGDALENE ODUNDO, potter

MAGDALENE ODUNDO, pots

44

Section Two

Talking in Tongues

This section opens with three chapters from our archive. In 1983/84 various women working in fields as diverse as acting, hairbraiding and fine art were encouraged to write about their craft for the 'original' BWCP Book. Although in some cases it took a bit of encouragement several women produced chapters. The three selected here by Yemi Morgan, Chila Burman and Meera Syal each speak volumes about the upswing and hopefulness of Blackwomens arts movements in the early eighties.

Yemi Morgan contextualises her craft as an African cultural tradition and shares with us anecdotes about the socialisation of womens skills into community activities. In establishing the Continuity of braiding from Ancient Egypt, through the diaspora, urban African, and up to the present day, we are offered an understanding of the politics of grooming. Ayoka Chenzira's "*Hairpiece*" a short animation film also addresses these issues and was screened during *Check It!* on the film evening.

Chila Burman continues to produce work in the nineties and seems to maintain the enthusiasm and sharp class analysis which is expressed in her contribution. Her work has been widely exhibited, she has worked on various community arts projects and recently had a solo show at the Horizon Gallery in London. She successfully inflects her imagery with acute political issues such as anti-nuke, the struggles in South Africa and the articulation of what it means to be an Asian woman artist. She has a fine sense of humour as we see from some of her installation work in particular. She exhibited in BWCP III at the *People's Gallery*, in London in 1985, and *The Thin Black Line*, ICA, London, 1985.

Meera Syal's award winning one woman show *One of us* was a great success on the Edinburgh Festival fringe. I saw the show on at least four occasions and she always maintained the same sharp certainty of presentation, the same commitment to her audience. She shares with us an insight into how she came to be an actress and how she made use of the contradictions she experienced growing up in Britain. Her skills have continued to expand and she is now established as an able and challenging actress.

Without the combination of these remarkable contributions, and Ingrid Pollard's documentary endeavours it is unlikely that *Passion* could have come into being, which is why they are printed here. As a contextulisation of the early stages of this book. It is remarkable that the women who agreed to participate never lost faith in the project. When things seemed to grind to a halt someone from somewhere would enquire as to how it was coming along and that would get it going again. Their optimism was infectious.

Lubaina Himid is a lecturer in Fine Art at Lancashire Polytechnic and has been the main force behind the flowering of Blackwomens Art in Britain. Her ground breaking shows *5 Black Women* at the Africa Centre, *Black Woman Time Now* and *The Thin Black Line* brought the work of artists such as Veronica Ryan, Sonia Boyce and Sutapa Biswas to a wider public, often taking the risk of giving women their first public exhibition. It is a testament to her vision as a curator and mentor that the Arts Council, Tate Gallery and various regional galleries have now bought works of art by Black women artists which Lubaina Himid herself commissioned. She worked as Assistant Curator to Jill Morgan at Rochdale Art Gallery 1988-90 and staged major shows by Donald Rodney, *Critical* and Claudette Johnson, *Pushing Back the Boundaries*.

No-one who saw her fabulous packing-case set for Paulette Randall's *Fishing* could forget her skills as a Theatre Designer. As an artist she has produced several of the decades most enduring art works in particular *Freedom and Change* (1984). *A Fashionable Marriage* (1986) and *The Ballad of the Wing* (1989). Her retrospective exhibition *New Robes for Mashulan* (1987) was groundbreaking in the documenting of an oevre by a Black woman in her '30s.

Bernardine Evaristo was a founding member of Theatre of Blackwomen. Her poetry has been published in *Beautiful Barbarians* (Onlywomen Press) and other publications. In the introduction to her poems she speaks of the politics of location and confronts the often painful, for Blackwomen, realities of being a tourist when travelling the world in search of self. She is currently compiling a collection of her poetry.

Maud Sulter was born in Glasgow, Scotland and currently lives in England. She is a writer and was awarded the Vera Bell Prize for Poetry in 1985 for her book *As A Blackwoman*. The poems published here are taken from *Zabat: Poetics of a Family Tree*, which was published by Urban Fox Press in 1989.

Performance art in Britain is something of closed shop for Blackwomen but **Delta Streete**, an artist who creates through movements, has taken the brave step of entering this hostile arena with pieces such as *The*

Quizzing Glass (1989) and *In The Deep* – a video performance (1990). The latter work was commissioned by The Elbow Room and premiered at the ICA.

Pat Agana is a writer and like many of the women in this book an activist. She is currently working on the issue of child sexual abuse and we are delighted to publish her speech here. Child sexual abuse is a subject which many Black female artists and writers have sought to expose and resolve in their work. Alice Walker's *The Color Purple*, Maud Sulter's *Zabat: Poetics of a family tree* and Sonia Boyce's *Mr. Close Friend of the Family* are just three works which articulate the complexity of the issue. Black feminists have been active in Rape Crisis, Anti-Pornography movements such as WAVAW and incest survivors groups. Many of the objectives which such campaigns have met have been, like the Civil Rights Movement, motivated by Black women. Sadly, their contribution has often been written out/invisibilised within predominately white womens groups. However autonomous organisation, *"seperatism in the course of health"* to paraphase Alice Walker, has enabled women such as Pat Agana to use her considerable skills and talents. Her poetry has also been published in *GEN: Blackwomen writer's supplement* (1985) and prose in various publications such as *FAN* and *Spare Rib* .

Nialah, are just one of the many Black female writing groups active around Britain. Their publications are now collectors' items and they continue to work, as a group in Manchester.

Olusola Oyeleye has carved a niche for herself in black theatre as a challenging director and community organiser. Her writing has been published in *GEN: Blackwomen Writer's Supplement* (1985) and various other publications including *FAN*. Her sister, Olufola, and mother, Mrs. Oyeleye, both contributed to the Blackwomen's issue of *FAN* writing on film and dress respectively. The family make regular visits to Nigeria.

Veena Stephenson is one of the new wave of Black feminist theorists. In her incisive essay she nips a few *Icons of Feminist Art Theory* in the ankle, such as the cultural piracy of Nancy Spero and the blatant exclusions of French Feminist Theory. Her own art illustrates her article. Veena Stephenson is employed by the Asian Women Writers Collective.

Dionne Sparks studied at Liverpool Polytechnic and continues to live and work in the city.

The **Asian Women Writers Collective** (then called a Group) took part in

47

their first public reading during the BWCP *Check It!* event at the Drill Hall in London in the summer of 1985. Since then they have gone from strength to strength. They have established an extensive network and have a new collection of writings on the way.

Olive Pollard is a keen gardener who has created two beautiful urban gardens in the past 30 years. Here she speaks about her skills with her daughter, Ingrid Pollard.

Nina Edge studied in Cardiff and continues to live and work there. Her work was included in BWCP III and she has exhibitied in exhibitions such as *Along The Lines of Resistance* and *Diverse Cultures*.

Patricia St. Hilaire was a founding member of Theatre of Blackwomen. Their groundbreaking productions included *Pyeyucca*.

Frederica Brooks studied at Middlesex Polytechnic. She was one of the exhibitors in *Out There Fighting,* an Elbow Room show, in 1988. She contributed to *Claudette Johnson: Pushing Back The Boundaries* Urban Fox Press 1990.

Maud Sulter

Yemi Morgan

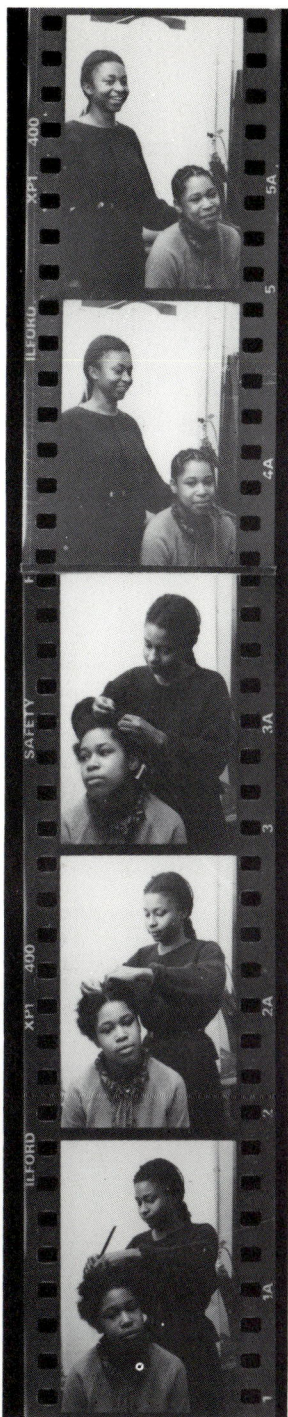

In the Shade of the Avocado Tree, the Girl Next Door and Me

Childhood memories. Grandmother's yard in Nigeria. Sitting under the huge avocado tree. Watching the girl next door plaiting head after head and eavesdropping on the latest gossip. Maintaining as unobtrusive presence as possible or I'd be sent away at the juicy bits. Wonderfully entertaining afternoons. Everyone off home with a truly individual style for a tip of a few pennies.

Gradually I started paying attention to the actual plaiting itself. I remember vividly my first plait. There I was fiddling with my hair as I watched television. I suddenly discovered that I could plait too. My sleeping sister was dragged from bed so I could practise on her hair. What a mess! But from there on there was no stopping me.

Saturdays in our house became the day all the girls in the neighbourhood came round to get their hair done for school. All very much a social event. Not the mainly commercial one it is nowadays, especially in the West.

My chosen career is science. While studying industrial science at Paisley College of Technology I found myself working occasionally in Hairlynks, a black hairdressing salon in Glasgow. Why Glasgow? My father is the Scottish equivalent of a Francophile. Having studied at Glasgow University nearly twenty-five years ago he fell in love with Scotland and as a result three of his children have studied there.

I prefer plaiting at home as there is less pressure to perform. I don't have the salon's reputation to protect. As a result I am more relaxed, work faster and enjoy the gossip like the old days. Plaiting in a salon puts a different emphasis on the activity altogether. From being a social event of little or no economic value it has become a commercial enterprise. It often provides a good percentage of the income of any salon offering the service.

Whether or not that is a good thing depends on your point of view. Plaiting is detached from its cultural aspects. The provision of a significant service to the community is done at a price as opposed to almost free.

49

Traditionally the art of hairdressing in Africa was a woman's skill. Practised almost exclusively by women and generally for women. Plaiting a head of hair can take any length of time. However most take an average of five hours to produce about seventy plaits. A five-hour plait in a salon will cost about £40. That might sound expensive but considering that a half-hour haircut costs about £6 it is not too bad*.

A SHORT HISTORY OF PLAITING

In most African societies plaiting originated for ceremonial purposes. Many have seen the Egyptian scrolls with plaited heads of hair, wigs and beards. These were worn by both women and men.

In the Yoruba tribe of Nigeria, of which I come, plaiting had a role to play in the traditional society. Like the medieval painters of Europe there was a framework of symbolism and style to be observed in this form of creative expression. Certain festivals had certain styles of hairdressing to observe.

Festival of the God of War
All plaits come from the base of the neck and were worked forward to the forehead.

The High Priestess of the River Goddess
Her plaits came up from the hairline to form a ponytail at the crown of her head.

Certain styles were reserved for different classes within the society.

The Wives of the King
Their plaits went straight from the front of the head to the nape of the neck. Slight variations on this style indicated the seniority of the wives.

In Yoruba society only women had their hair plaited. However in other societies, such as the Hausa in northern Nigeria, men also had plaits.

As time went by these restrictions on plaiting were loosened.

Esi Sagay, a sister Nigerian, has produced a book called *African Hairstyles* which documents its history and development across the entire continent of Africa.

TYPES OF PLAITING

Any pattern that can be drawn can be translated into a plaited sculpture on the human head.

Traditionally hair is woven, cornrowed or threaded.

Weaving and Cornrowing

Both are interchangeable each being the inversion of the other. The hair is parted into strips. The process starts with three portions from the base of the roots. To weave, the three portions are passed over the other in the order 1, 2, 3, 1, 2, 3 with 1 being the middle portion. Hair is picked up as the plait progresses to the end of the strip. The plait is finished by plaiting all remaining hair at the end with no more picking up. In cornrowing the portions of hair are passed underhand.

Threading

The whole head is divided into sections. Each section is wound tightly with thread to give a rope effect.

Two modern variations are single plaits and bobtailing.

Single plaits

The hair is sectioned. Each section is divided into three and plaited <u>away</u> from the head to the end. Beads may be added.

Bobtailing

Bobtails combine the principles of plaiting and threading. Again the hair in each portion is sectioned but this time each portion is divided into four. Three portions are plaited as before. Then the fourth portion is wound continuously around the plait to give an overall dreadlock effect.

CHOOSING THE STYLE

The beauty of plaits is the fact that they can be styled to suit any shape of head or hairtype as long as the hair is a couple of inches long.

False hair is used to extend the length of plaits on short hair. Extensions woven into short hair gives the impression of length without having to put on a wig. It is also invaluable when plaiting white European hair as it eliminates the problem of sealing the end of the plait. Burning off the end seals the plait preventing it unravelling as straight hair has a tendency to do.

Most of my clients in the salon want a lot of plaits hanging down to which they can add beads. This is a very simple style which just follows the natural hairline.

The versatility of plaits is often highlighted at salon shows. Fans wing across the head, T-shapes, multicoloured thread mix with beads. Even a bridal veil created from plaits which can be worn forward or back. Imagination and patience are all you need to create these beautiful works of art.

PLAITING AS A POLITICAL STATEMENT
With the advent of straighteners and perms for Blackpeople's hair, plaiting went out of fashion in urban areas of Africa.

In the USA, however, the afro hair styles of the Black Panthers and others involved in the cultural consciousness-raising of the Civil Rights Movement developed into plaited styles. Black was beautiful for true. Afro-Americans had continued cornrowing in diaspora. However, they would cover their heads with head-rags or, later, wigs. The White-Americans did not approve. It passed on the heads of children but was 'unsuitable' for adults.

As the skill was still in practice it was a readily available way of redefining a cultural tradition within Black-America, which had been denied its rightful place and recognition as a part of their African cultural heritage.

This re-evaluation was followed by a popularisation of these styles by international celebrities such as Cicely Tyson, the actress, and Stevie Wonder, the musician. As a result modern reinterpretation of old styles have worked their way back to Africa.

Overall, plaiting is now very much in vogue in urban areas both in Africa and abroad. The beauty of African hair sculpture and the fact that once complete it looks after itself is, I believe, the reason plaits have been popular for at least 5,000 years.

* These are 1983 prices!

Chila Kumari
Burman

Don't Rush Me ... Hiya Sisters and Hey Mr Big Stuff

To speak not from head to head but from heart to heart. To utter not a word that is not experienced, lived through. To speak not about something or other but to speak simply oneself. That is what I shall try in what follows.

"Why all this fussin and a fightin" ... Rita Marley ... "Total destruction the only solution"...

I was born in Liverpool six-and-a-half pounds and very hairy. My mum and dad, who are both Hindu-Punjabi, came to this country in the '50s. Me mum is amazing. To think that she brought us up here. Even gave birth to some of us without knowing a word of English. That's really something else. Me dad is a brilliant tailor and a really wise man. He taught us about love and respect. He used to be a magician on stage eating fire and glass. Like a true professional he would never tell us how he did it. Yeah truly Magic. They're both dead loving and caring like me brothers and sister; Achar, Ashan, Ashok and Ashra. Must also mention Paul, me nephew, who's a genius.

We are all quite talented and creative in our family. My sister acted before, me brothers all create – make music, write and live it up. So we all share our interests and ideas.

Our goal is freedom.

I went to school in Bootle and to three art schools. In all of them I did mostly printmaking – excellent. Etching, silkscreen, lithography and mono-printing. There were hardly any facilities at the school but you could still manage to make monoprints from old spuds or even by inking some different parts of yer body up then pressing up against the paper or screen ... magic. Now I've mostly been doing photo-etching and making photo-montages.

There were some hassles at college from some staff and students. Some were really racist, ignorant, sexist and stupid. There was a lot of sexism. Totally out of order things like "Cor she's a good mover" when you were trying to ink up your lithography plates. Not on. I'll ink them up one day!

53

Racism was always there hidden and institutionalised. Occasional attacks like "You dumb black" a variation on "You dumb blond". Both totally pathetic and ridiculous.

There were attacks on your work. What you were supposed to be saying. All male staff. There was a kind of fear. I was lucky to have a personal tutor who at least listened.

There was corruption, competition, divisiveness. All this trouble and strife and messiness started to get me angrier and madder. All these thoughts, feelings, objective and subjective, political, unconscious and conscious ideas, were put into action. So you can see through my work that I began to expose all this. It has helped me to untangle and understand what was going on in all this madness. It had to be done. Otherwise I would have gone bonkers. I was lucky to have access to all those facilities to allow me to create these photomontages. That is where creating is dead important. You release all and start to live and breath again. It is a MANIFESTATION OF LIFE.

I want to see a move towards a demystification of art from within the system. Everyone should be allowed the space and opportunity to realise their full potential and what they've got. Not just the privileged or those who go through the crazy system of school and Higher education.

Some people scorn art. It never seems to be understood. Yet there's a lot of exciting stuff around. In performance, video, film, painting and music. Creating is a way of getting in touch with reality. With oneself and nature.

In the last institution I was in, the photography department sent me a letter saying "…it should be understood that the department cannot deal with private work of the nature you left in the department recently. It was of a *personal* nature." Why all this fussin' and a fightin'? Let it be. I just wanted peace but there was corruption breaking out all over the place.

Don't Mash up Creation. In the prints I try to be dead honest and let it all hang out. *Wisdom oh Wisdom.* It's easier said than done. I am aware of the contradictions and the high cost of living, let it be. When you let it all hang out even if you think something's not worth drawing, writing, dancing, shouting about, do it. 'Cos everything's worth doing. No-one has the right to say what is good or bad. The way of seeing is the way of

54

being. It would be good to see a demystification of art within the present system ... forward sisters. Freedom is our goal.

The pictures shown here are all kinda different. Indian women, women under apartheid, anti-nuke stuff. The ideas, issues, plus my own culture have determined the content and form. They represent a consciousness and a cultural response to the kind of institution I was in and what was going on both inside and on the outside.

If and when I use images of men I try to subvert them or put a new perspective on them. In expressing personal thoughts I try to create something that is more direct and harmonious thus bringing about an awareness of what is going on. It reflects the changes the women's movement has attached to the personal in the political world. They both merge.

I would like to see my work as an inspiration and bringing about an awareness of what's going on. It's kinda social, political and real. Everything's political really. The prints describe what I feel. Nasty things, anger, fear, suffering, madness. Like in *One Race the Human Race* the gas masks symbolize war and anti-nuke stuff. I want to create new, strong, direct, powerful, natural, balanced, real creative images of Black and Asian women so as to challenge the stereotypical assumption the media has. Especially of Asian women.

I produced some images for a tape-slide that was made by sisters about challenging these issues. It's called *Stepping Out of Frame* by Amina Patel and Laxmi Jamfdagni.

When making pictures and drawings I take my own photographs and collect others from magazines, books and the like for ideas and information. It isn't easy creating but good fun. Art shouldn't be a rat-race or competitive. It's easy to fall into the trap of being competitive. Like it requires an almost superhuman purity of heart not to, but having exhibitions isn't everything. It's what you put into it from your heart that counts. *Don't mash up Creation*. Have to repeat this quote from an ace book called *The Zen of Seeing and Drawing* which our Billy showed me. "Art is the unspoilt core in everyone, before being choked by schooling, conditioning and training, until the artist within shrivels up and is forgotten. Art is that which, despite all, gives hope. Simply a matter of being, living."

The word 'artist' is a verb rather than a noun. Creating is like feeding yourself, spoon by spoon, filling up your belly. Then you begin to beam and shine and love. It's real. Direct painting to reality.

At college you are sometimes taught to believe that *one* has to have an exhibition every year to prove whatever it is that *one* is driven to prove. I began to think about this. Is this really what it's all about? The more you think about it the more phoney you realise it is. Creating is more than therapy.

Being an Asianwoman in and now out of college isn't easy. There are stacks of obstacles but I try to keep living and moving forward. Naturally and peacefully. It's a tough world and I try to be aware of my own contradictions as much as possible … we can clean it up sisters … don't mash up Creation. We can transcend and transform. Challenge and reveal these issues. Like the imbalance of power relations that exists between men and women. Especially violence against women. Using all mediums. Like film, writing, talking, print, singing, sound, science, dancing and living. Then the world would really be a better place to live in – nice – one – mash – up – sisters.

It ain't easy surviving and creating. To quote Rita Marley again "There's always someone out there to put you down. Your heart gotta be strong."

To all creating and loving sisters we ARE strong and dynamic. For ever and ever …

Namaste Benji's (Goodbye sisters).

Meera Syal

Finding My Voice

The tension mounted as the director cast his critical eye over the audition-ees lined up nervously in front of him. "I want to say that this has been a difficult decision to make. Okay. First the White Queen…" And as the cast list for class 6's production of *Alice Through the Looking Glass* was read out a certain precocious seven year-old listened to the announcements with disbelief. "The Rose – the bleedin rose! Ten lines and a stupid frilly costume. But I know I'm the best actress in the class. Why haven't I got a bigger role?" The director (alias the woodwork teacher) took her aside and said kindly, "Now then Feroza, we can't have an Alice with a brown face, can we?" and I knew my battle had begun.

When I confessed a secret longing to become an actress no-one was very surprised. Experience had taught me that performing as the class clown prevented me being forcibly cast as the class coon. My most effective form of self-defence was not physical but mimicry, joke telling and face pulling. And it proved to be a fundamentally theatrical talent. Moreover, an adolescence split uncomfortably between my attention grabbing displays at school and a lovingly protective though enclosed existence at home had endowed me with a schizophrenic ability to roleswap which any actor would admire.

Lying on my bed and burning to be gone was probably one of the less self-indulgent lines I composed during my brief phase as a songwriter. I would pluck out *My-baby's-gone-and-died-on-me* ballads on my guitar. Yet it sums up the frustrations of one Asian teenager stirred by daydreams of fame and fortune but too young, and perhaps too scared, to recognise these dreams as non-verbal cries for independence, self-expression, emancipation. Being now older and hopefully wiser I can understand how my desire to act was inevitably connected to my growing awareness of my identity as an Asian woman in this country. After all, both processes encouraged the development of a positive, individual voice and it was only with time that I realised both voices were speaking the same language.

Had I waited for the education system to provide me with vocalisation I would be silent still.

Drama at school was limited to the annual Shakespeare extravaganza. Encouraging that kind of declamatory acting in which the accent is

perfect and the feeling nil. The thought of drama school was attractive in a romantic sort of way. However, my parents with the inherent Asian anxiety for me to have an *education* were keen for me to go into Higher education. So, at the age of eighteen I left home for the first time to read for an English and Drama degree at Manchester University.

Hooray for immigrant caution! My four years spent in this active department provided me with a range of experience from community theatre to classical farce which worked wonders for my confidence and, most importantly, for my self-awareness.

Consequently, I never regretted not going to drama school. Within such an environment, with its emphasis on stage technique, I fear that my gradual exploration of my Asian identity would have been relegated to an unhealthy second place. With each new role I tackled at University I was forced to consider not so much *how* I was performing but *who* exactly was up there on stage. In a classical role I would be quite simply Feroza the performer. Colourless and cultureless. Adapting herself to the requirements of a verse drama. In a community theatre show I would be very much Feroza the Asian woman. Using her role to make some statement about both colour and culture. It was the old schizophrenic role swapping of my adolescence only this time it did not take place on the private stage of teenage fantasy but on a very real and public stage where I had to take responsibility for the statements being made through this apparent playacting.

I began to understand the crucial connection between my creative capacities and my political awareness. A symbolic process in which development in one would feed and encourage growth of the other. In this way feelings which might not be released in physical rehearsal during the day would be discovered, identified and released by combined effect with the books I read at night.

Having started off with the accepted landmarks of feminist thought; Germaine Greer's *Female Eunuch*, Kate Millett's *Sexual Politics* and Simone de Beauvoir's *Second Sex*, I finally located works which dealt specifically with the Asian woman's experience. Such as Gail Omvedt's *We Will Smash This Prison* and the brilliant and painful *Finding A Voice* by Amrit Wilson. As I began to understand more about myself as an Asian woman my powers of expression and confidence on stage became more defined. Fired by this process of self-discovery I had found my cause and my creativity with it.

The problem of schizophrenia still remained unsolved. I found myself torn between playing parts which would stretch my acting abilities to their fullest capacity at the expense of ignoring my feelings as an Asian performer and those roles which would allow the Asian in me to speak, such as in community theatre shows, but inevitably these roles sometimes reduced my performance to that of a didactic mouthpiece. Where was the script that could combine these two sides of my personality, which could express my feelings as an Asian woman in a skilful and challenging way? I soon realised how many untold stories lay silent on the lips of Asian women in this country (Britain). Silenced by both their inability to verbalise their frustrations in a society which regards them as second-class citizens and a theatre and media in which the Asian presence is minimal and often merely nominal. I wished to give voice to this silence in the best way I knew. Through my acting.

Out of this resolution emerged a piece of drama in which I felt both artistically challenged and politically fulfilled – *One of Us*. It is a forty-five minute one-woman show dealing with the experiences of Nishi a young Asian teenager who has left her Birmingham home in order to become an actress. The play itself is set at Nishis first audition.

"Am I late?" she gasps as she makes her entrance on roller skates. The prawn on her hat; part of the required uniform at *Prawn Fantasy* the restaurant where she works, wobbling as she speaks.

By gradually building up a relationship with the audience whom she addresses as her fellow auditionees she plays out selected scenes from her recent past. These glimpses into her life illustrate how and why she has abandoned her home and with it, apparently, any allegiance towards her culture and community.

One Of Us has been described as "A comic *Pilgrims Progress*" (Naseem Khan, City Limits) and "The transformation of a second-rate actress to an artist of unshakeable dignity and grace" (The Times), but the reviews have always stressed the truth of the piece. The piece is all these things because its creative expression is powered by a need to convey some deeply felt and largely ignored experiences of an Asian woman living in Britain. It is political theatre at its most powerful.

The play emerged through my collaboration with a close writer-friend, Jacqui Shapiro, who was studying on a writer's bursary in the drama department at Manchester whilst I was involved with my final exams. I knew that I had a wealth of experience and material which I wished to convey but I lacked the objectivity and craft necessary to fashion raw emotion into a piece of performable theatre. Similarly Jacqui wanted to tackle monologue form knowing it to be a notoriously difficult genre for a writer to handle with originality and force. And so the partnership began. Eight weeks of involved production. An hour's worth of improvised material might produce, perhaps, ten minutes which could be set down. Jacqui would complete this task at home before the next day's session.

Considering this intensively personal method of composition it is perhaps not surprising that Nishi emerges as a perfect alter-ego of my own personality. She expresses the naïve unselfconscious desires to become a superstar which preoccupy the teenagers she follows in her favourite television programme *Fame*. Nishi is equally unashamed in her condemnation of a culture and family-life which she feels makes the fulfillment of those dreams impossible. She falls back on the device which I used to employ in the past. Humour.

Witness, for instance, how she wickedly parodies the areas of her life in which this pull of two cultures has the most painful consequences. About her father's strict surveillance over her as she works in the family shop – "He's so embarrassing. Can't even speak English properly." and the attitude of the customers towards her in the restaurant where she works – "I know all about you Eastern women. You make out that you're all virgins but underneath you're hot beds of passion..."

As Nishi is continually confronted by images of the racism of the white society she so desperately wishes to belong to it; the society she has totally abandoned her own community for in the hope that it will accept her, the humour dies down. The confrontation reaches its climax in Nishi's meeting with her now militant mother who is picketing the factory where she now works. The protest is against unfair conditions and wages. This provides an ironic comparison to her daughter's daydreams of stardom and fame.

Up to this point Nishi's behaviour has followed patterns similar to my own. She expresses the guilt I have often felt at my ignorance of my own culture yet she is also a sympathetic-enough character to demonstrate how easy it is to fall into the trap of self-dissolution undergone in the name of integration.

The end of the play is something of an expiation for both me and Nishi. When she finally reaches the acting audition with which the play began, she is halfway through her prepared song and dance routine from the musical *My Fair Lady* when the cultural tightrope, she has been walking throughout the play, finally snaps. The cute Cockney ditty is abandoned as she joyfully stamps out the steps of a Punjabi folk dance barely remembered from family parties at home in the past.

And so Nishi makes the first tentative steps towards some reconciliation with her culture. Nishi has failed her audition but won the initial battle to rediscover and retain some pride in her identity as an Asian woman. This is always the point in the play where I feel at my most powerful and expressive as a performer. Nishi begins by resenting her difference and ends by realising that difference as both her strength and her lifeline. If I can hold onto this throughout my career as a performer I will be satisfied.

LUBAINA HIMID, 'Three Women at the Fountain'
(detail) remade 1989

LUBAINA HIMID **Mapping:** A Decade Of Black Women Artists 1980-1990

Being the first has its triumphs, keeping going is where the hard work begins. If we really believed we were the first black women to call ourselves artists we would have an excuse to give up, we were not, we are the continuum. We are part of an enormous international movement which stretches far back in time.

I am often asked to prove this ancestry, my usual reaction is to make another piece of work or to organise another exhibition. Being a black woman artist in the eighties was a very public thing. This high profile was linked to several key economic and political shifts. The late seventies had seen the coming to power of a very English conservatism, one which promised to do the work of the extremist right through the ballot box. The children of the workers from the Caribbean were leaving school and going/not going on to higher education. The police were beginning to be paid more, and promised more, they had to deliver. The left wing was very vociferous in its opposition, however as the decade wore on it became more apparent that this was ineffectual. The women's movement had become a more complicated issue. The work of the Africans in regaining the power of their own countries had been forgotten and blurred. The Civil Rights movement in the States had been marketed as different from here, so that we were led to believe that the most important thing to happen in 1968 was the white student protests in Paris. So the period of the early '80s was one of half remembered details, autodidactic research and struggle on the streets for the black woman. I believe we appeared to be being offered choices and the chance to conform.

This illusion was both public and private; the right was saying, be a second class citizen and there will be a place for you, serve your purpose as the invisible oil in the machine and all will be well; the left on the other hand used the black person as a breath of life, a reviving elixir, a dose of sugar, a splash of colour. The music needed us, the women's movement needed us, simplistic left-wing politics needed us as the working class after all were not playing the game. Publishing certainly needed us, women's publishing could not have drawn its second breath without us. Now in the nineties the art world does not appear to need us so it is difficult to see how and why they let us in back then. The answer lies in much of the preceding paragraph. *Public Art galleries* in Britain are of course political animals. They are funded by and through the workings of political parties. *The funding bodies* have tended to be officiated by the liberal left fighting a losing battle against the ruling right. This simplistic use of the terms left and right is inadequate as a description but these are the labels of self-naming. *Art schools* are also liberal establishments dedicated ostensibly to equality and human rights. These three arenas then, at the beginning of the eighties, presented themselves as safe havens, apparently offering real choices for the black woman who wishes to be an artist.

Can the equation be as simple as; The government wants black people to be quiet, so when we justifiably revolt against state terrorism it provides money for us to be creative and expand our ideas prettily. The money then goes to the funders (- The Arts Council and the Regional Arts Associations -) who cannot give the money directly to us and so give it to the galleries to give to us. The government wants us quiet so when we 'riot' it provides money for us to be creative and expand our ideas prettily, the money goes to the polytechnics who make sure that every year there is *a* black student in painting, or print making. If the first part equals the sum of the second part is the answer that we were used? Did we imagine we had choices? Did we, despite the revolutionary nature of our work, actually conform, keep quiet, stay in our place? Or did we seize a moment, communicate with each other and set a pattern in remotion. I think that only the next twenty years will tell, but in order not to repeat the exercise in order not to re/re/invent the wheel it is perhaps important to outline the chronology of the work and exhibitions of the black woman artist in the eighties. Not as a list but as a series of events and coincidences, of opportunities lost and taken, of careers made and destroyed. A huge amount of energy was used in those years. I would like it not to have been wasted, I can see with the glorious benefit of hindsight how things could have been better, but I can also see that lies were told to lead us astray, some of the best people believed those lies.

Each action in this particular mapping had five parts to its sum. Black women artists I would posit never moved without these elements being essential to the action. These are Funding, Education, Galleries, Art History, and Audience.

Let us begin with money I will have to end with it and mention it all the time but it lies at the source of much of the debate around what it is to be an artist and the artists place in any society. Britain has a worldwide reputation for spending minute amounts on art, both as government policy and as a nation of shoppers. The British it seems do not want to enhance their surroundings with original pieces of creativity made by a professional person, whose job and joy it is to be an artist. The British do not think that the environment can be made spectacularly uplifting by the presence of a piece of modern sculpture, it prefers for its outdoor enjoyment the statue and the car. Art is thought of, or so we are led to believe, as an additional luxury item provided when and only when everything else has been bought. This placed the Funder in a very powerful position, at least in the eighties. We had a situation where the only place that you could get cash to make an innovative or radical piece of art, or to stage a supposedly political exhibition was either the Arts Council, the local authority, or the regional arts body, whose money was given to them by the government. The government, you remember, was trying to keep black people from loudly complaining in the streets about the essentials that were being denied us and so there was money for black people making art. It was a very small amount of money, much less than it cost. For instance the early black women's shows that I curated existed on almost nothing. *5 Black women at the Africa Centre* was staged without a fee to either selector or artists. The Africa Centre gallery itself was not successful either in gaining financially from showing the work. This was due to their non relationship to the regional arts body who had no comprehension of Africans making art. There was no money at all for the selector or artists of the exhibition *Black Woman Time Now* at Battersea Arts Centre. No money for transport or a catalogue. The Arts Centre itself however gained enormous reputation by staging the show and the wider festival. *The Thin Black Line* at the ICA was blessed with a little pocket money, each artist had about eleven foot of wall space and if they used extra material there was a budget of thirty pounds. I received £250 for selecting the show, a task which took the best part of six months. The GLC had threatened to withdraw its considerable contribution to the ICA if something black did not appear in that financial year. There was a catalogue but more of that later. It must be made clear that during this time and still today, extra money was given to established galleries if they wanted to stage black exhibitions. No questions were asked of them! It was a way of getting money into the coffers. A gallery could request money for these shows and then spend the money they already had to fund the exhibitions they 'really believed in'. I sat on arts panels and I read applications, I went to exhibitions, the evidence is there. Money from funding bodies very rarely goes to the individual artist but GLA hung on to this section for as long as it could. It is extraordinary how many times a black artists work was 'new' to the panel. Most people selected work by particular artists when they had seen it before and knew the artist. Another pitfall was that the black artist made work in whatever space could be found, 'the studio' was unusual. A studio visit was therefore often a disaster, an intrusion into the black woman's home, exposing an 'unprofessional' environment.

Work by black women artists has been bought by individuals and by the public collections. I could however list the works, and their creators, and the collections without having to do any research whatsoever. We have had to rely on our friends and relatives and our ever encouraging audience to buy the work, we have not been made rich yet by the gratefully received efforts. The teaching profession which is the method by which most recognised British artists make a living is one that is, shall we say, curiously, closed to us.

Money then is a little difficult to pin down. Commissions are rare, one notable exception being Rochdale Art Gallery in Lancashire, England. It is quite hard to make work that challenges dominant visual expressions, television and advertising, with the tools of pencil, brush, paper, crayon, cloth. The challenge was rather like that game; paper-stone-scissors and we rose to it.

Having touched on the art educational establishment I will now try to make clear our relationship to it. Those of us who went to art school are indeed privileged. We have degrees and the opportunity to name ourselves as artists. We have had time and resources to explore ideas.

Of this there is no doubt. What a shock it was though to realise that the art school was not a safe place, free of racism and sexism and all this from men, many of whom claimed to be heroes of the working class!

Why and how did so many women during the 1980s in British art schools become undermined, undervalued, discouraged and in some cases defeated. Time after time I have been told by tutors and by the women artists themselves that they would rather work at home than go into college. Black women students have been punished for this action time and time again. They produced the work but the public arena of the open studio remained a problematic environment. This story of the atmosphere in art schools has been told to me by almost every black woman artist I know. Not only by the ones that do not make it to the end of the course.

A great deal of the teaching work we were given in the last decade was a result of a black woman student, known to be talented, who simply refused to attend college, having realised that the tuition on offer was working against her creative methods. It was not always the radical student who gave up.

There are at the time of writing only a handful, by which I mean perhaps five, black women in teaching posts in Arts Schools in Britain. Our role as Blackwomen artists when we leave college is to rescue departments and tutors from themselves and each other. We are called in to add a touch of 'difference' to a diet of similar. To perform. To give an hour long slide show followed by tutorials. I have been asked to do 13 tutorials in one-and-a-half days. I have been asked to do an hour long seminar for £18 and no expenses, although I would have to travel from the North to London. I have known a black woman who taught for a term in a photography department and was then turned down for even an interview when a part-time job became vacant in that department the next year. The post filled by a white woman. Some of these things are illegal, all of them are exhausting and prevent the making of artwork.

If the artist wants to be thought of as a professional, by her family, her community, and by the funders and the art schools who provide a way of earning a living, if she wants to enter art history and be seen to have made a contribution, she must show her work in the Art Gallery. The art gallery is run by a small number of curators who work their way from one gallery to another seeking promotion and the enhancement of an international reputation. For example a person may start life in the art world, related to someone already in a position of relative power, they may start as an assistant in one gallery and after two years or so, go on to run another gallery. The residing encumbrant moves on to yet another gallery and a relationship is set up. Most of the current crop of British curators have worked in at least one or two other galleries, it is a very small group. There is no such thing as constructive networking, only the enhancing of reputation, and the compromise brought on by a funding crisis or the inability to tour your favourite exhibition. This you may say is fair, and anyhow it is the way in which the world works, true, then let us not pretend it is anything else!

Let us not pretend to care about the artist, the community, the audience, the children. We have already identified that *the gallery* has shown the work of the black woman artist in the last decade, but scientific tests will prove that very rarely is she represented by a body of work. The pervading impression is therefore of a great proliferation of exhibitions of black artists work, huge numbers of artists, but no real expanding of an individuals boundaries. There have been no more than 8 solo exhibitions by black women in major galleries in the last decade. Five of these have taken place in one gallery in a span of four years. There have been a large number of establishment endorsed mega-shows. With more than fifty artists in each, who can remember the names let alone the work? It looked impressive on the funding application. It is a fact that you cannot successfully tour a black woman's solo exhibition. Four of those 'no more than eight', were only seen in their originating gallery. The mega-show however has great bargaining power, and can even earn the money back that the gallery may have been forced to spend to begin with. These were the conditions in the eighties. There is now a fantastic and fool proof reason for the gallery not to show the work of the black woman artist; sponsorship. I have heard a curator gleefully announce that she was now forced to bow to the wishes of the sponsor. I have a suspicion that the sponsor is not being asked to sponsor radical work. That the curator assumes the terms of the contract precludes it.

So what of art history? We, as black women artists, are a part of an integral part of art history not only recent history but we belong up there with the important influences on world art. This may seem rather eccentric but the facts are there to be seen, even today, in places where art is important but where galleries are not. European/American art history has at best done us a great dis-service, at worst we are being stifled and smothered; stopped. It is assumed that because Brancusi made the work that he did, that the bronzes of Benin were made by men. It is supposed that because we don't tend to have solo exhibitions every two years that we do not have the capabilities to produce the work. Art history means being written about in books or at the very least well respected art journals. Art historians do not visit the 'studio' until they have seen the exhibition. Art books are expensive to produce and bought by the few. The black woman artist is not a very safe bet for profit, as she does not have many solo shows. In recent years she has appeared collectively as a footnote in the chronicling of the Feminist Art Movement. The black woman, her art and politics was an integral part of this movement but there are not, in Britain at least, the solo shows to prove it. The same art history, at least in terms of the historians reputation, is also made in the art journal. In Britain there are perhaps ten art journals, thus far no one is risking their reputation on a black woman artist. No one who teaches in an art history department, that is, no one who writes books, or footnotes us *en masse* that is. We cannot rely on newspapers or style magazines, we are not musicians after all. We can insist on catalogues when we do show work and we can expect the odd 250 words in a listing publication.

There is an area pitted with potholes in which art history and education are hand in hand with the gallery, the artist often trips up. I speak of the Education Slide Pack, this little gem is funded by the gallery and consists of slides of artwork, which are then bought by the educational establishment, used by the art history department, and so depriving you of your one hour slide talk performance. The student does have the benefit of seeing the artwork but it is interpreted by the art historian, who will not risk a reputation by airing this opinion in a public place. We can of course become the art historian, much as we can become the curator and the art school teacher, but what becomes of the artist? There are magazines that have grown in the last decade that name themselves as black art journals and the miracle is that they keep going, they are carefully watched over by the funders, no cheating now? The fact that black creativity often crosses the boundaries of art, literature music and performance is a problem for a funding panel whose name is visual arts. What happens when we do decide to put down the crayon for a moment and theorise a little on the strategies and directions; and we do it as black women and we write about black women because that is what is important to us. Is this art history? What if it is not in a publication blessed with being art historically sound? Is separatism allowed if it is black and not white? Will the publication be reprinted or will it, like the ICA catalogue for *The Thin Black Line*, have to wait four years until UFP reprints? In 1988 Maud Sulter and I co-edited an issue of FAN, a reprint was promised, further funding was assured on the strength of it, but it is now out of print. The publications in which we are colourful footnotes run and run.

Audience a legend in its own lunch-hour is what has kept the black woman artist in business all this time, and it always will be. So long as she makes the work for herself, other versions of herself will take the time and the trouble to trek the land in search of the latest, or the earliest work of the black woman artist. The excellent thing about the art gallery is that, at least for the moment, anyone is allowed in through the door. Sometimes you need to pay, sometimes you need to be able to climb stairs, and you always are required to have partial sight at least. This state of affairs means that whatever your colour, or political leanings, or your age, you can see the work of the black woman artist as long as it is on the wall. In the last ten years here there have been many occasions, the black art conference in Wolverhampton in 1982; the *Thin Black Line* seminar at the ICA in 1985 and, on many occasions, at the Black Art Gallery, in numerous workshops in galleries up and down the country and of course in many an art school seminar room, where the question of whether we make work for an exclusive audience is debated. I would argue that we do, whether we admit it or not and whether we succeed or not. That audience is ourselves. It is obvious that if artist and galleries treat their audience with the respect they deserve (galleries have great difficulty with this one) only good debate and exchange can result.

69

Art is about dialogue and there are many entry points. Questions of colour and light are as important to grapple with by audience and artist as are arguments of representation and its politics. There are discussions of history and its effect on the history of art which can continue long after the exhibition has ended. In other words if the work that has been made has been successful it has been work with a variety of entry points for a wide range of people. There is little point making work to please everyone all the time. That is a thankless and ultimately hopeless task. If work addresses a particular audience this does not mean it excludes all other audience. Galleries need audiences now to prove that they are popular places to be. To prove that they deserve the funding they get. There is nothing a council official hates more than an empty municipal gallery. Many people who visit municipal galleries like them to be quiet places of contemplation. The supermarket and bank, the dole office and the television are noisy enough. School children bump up the audience figures, so methods are devised to bring them in. Do not make work that may offend children. Audience is an anonymous mass, with a bureaucratic link to the money provided for art. The education of the person in the street, its relationship to the gallery, its demand for an art with a history, is a dangerous thing. It is not real. Audience is real people, spending real and sometimes precious time, looking at work that has been made in order to foster dialogue and make change.

The results of the actions made by black women artists are there, plain to see. Many are making work on the cheap, their work too cranky to be taken seriously. A few others are making work with inadequate but more real time funding. These latter are making a contribution too serious to be ignored but also too serious to be taken seriously. In other words it is fine for black women to be making work that is constructed from odd bits and pieces, it jazzes up the odd 'serious lefty show'. When colleagues of these women hustle and work for funds, to build an oeuvre that does indeed challenge the dominant values in media and representation, there is consternation and whispering. But this is an easy analysis, the bottom line is that this work does not get shown. The gallery is frightened. What will the sponsor say, for we are now in the thrall of the sponsor and not the mayor. The sponsor I would posit is delighted, he likes a smooth finished product which reeks of the future, and has an entry point for him in terms of beauty and professionalism. It is the gallery which is frightened. The gallery is run by the liberal. If the black woman artist makes work for the gallery curator with just the right touches of guilt inducement pseudo-eroticism and victim posturing she will not only get it shown but she will sell it to public collections. It has been done, it works. It is of no use to black women. They have all (the women you read about and see on the walls and even those you don't) gone through the zones that I set out in the beginning. It is how they have negotiated the hills and the rivers, how they have known what is over the next mountain and whether they have cared or not that will make clear the future.

The money situation is making a serious shift as we enter the nineties. The Arts Council is devolving much of its power and money to the regions. This does *not* mean the huge sums it gives the London galleries, but the inadequate sums it doled out if you promised to trek your show to more than three galleries. The regional arts associations are being merged with each other and none of the officers, who after all are the real human beings that give out the money, are quite sure of their own salary. As the decade goes on it will be easier to see what this means for the black woman artist, but it is obvious that the less money there is to go round the less is available for radical intervention of the spectacular kind. I have mentioned that the sponsor is now a player in the game, it would be too easy to say that none will sponsor the work of black women artists, but the middle negotiator between the artist and the sponsor has to have the nerve to ask. In the latter part of the '80s even the top people in funding were nervous of having to risk this. Those people who had got used to brow beating councillors and were contemptuous of them, are now finding it very difficult to have the same attitude to the business sector, of whom they are often equally disparaging. We could think much, much more of selling the work that we make. For this, in Britain, we need to be part of the stable of the commercial gallery. The private gallery has international links, takes around fifty per cent in commission, makes sure you appear in the right open shows. The John Moore's in Liverpool, the Portrait Show at the National Portrait Gallery London etc. They should make sure that you get good media coverage and they will sell your work even if you are a black woman, as long as they have thought in advance who to sell it to, and indeed how to market it. Exotic, erotic, radical, cranky. The prices they will be able to command for your work will be, should be, higher than anything you could charge. The artist cannot fight this particular marketing arena, you are either in it or you are not, no half measures.

In the past we have seen that black women have not been sought after to teach in higher education in the arts but perhaps now the line and the strategy is changing? The student in the polytechnic that is a company is now the client. Will we see a time when the student demands the teacher it wants? Will they choose the black woman? Will they be allowed to? I have to say that much of the teaching work that came my way did so because *students* had seen my work in exhibitions and wanted to meet me and discuss *their* work. Given the current changing climate in education, the arena in which many British artists earn the time and money to paint, nothing is clear vis-à-vis the future. I have a suspicion however that when black women are allowed to teach in art education in any numbers that the days of the creative degree will be over. Black people are not usually given a slice of the pie until there are only crumbs to be had. It has happened in local government, and it has happened in arts funding.

If the showing of work is linked to finance, and we have very little of it, what is there to do? The thing not to do is give up. We have to keep making the work, somehow. Easy to say. The catch is that if you have no work to show you have no work to show. So, however small it is, however cheap it is, however cranky it is, keep making the work. The work will eventually work for you. If you have mega ideas make mega plans. Do not let the ideas stop coming because you do not think anyone will ever show it. Make small versions of big ideas. Do not be surprised when your good ideas are stolen, (sometimes even by overly ambitious blackwomen), this is the lot of the black woman artist, you are in good company. Know the place where you would like to show, keep an eye on what they do. Never stop looking at the things that inspire you.

It has been depressing not to have been immortalised in the coffee table book or the radical journal. It has forced some of us into being publishers when we would rather be looked after and cosseted by some non-existant-caring-lucrative-other. It seems this was not to be. Even when eminent art historians do vouch for ones artistic talents, genius even, the British Council will not fund us to go to America or Europe to give lectures to accompany exhibitions, even when one is the only British artist in a show. Not British enough. Not born here. Too radical.

An encouraging view of the world is that one, as a black woman, is not a minority. On a global scale our audience is huge, rich, and varied. Links can and must be made between ourselves and other black women who are creating new work.

Bernardine
Evaristo

Thinking Around the Poems

During the past five years my writing has been greatly influenced by travelling. Journeys to other countries liberate my creativity. I feed hungrily on the sight, sound, smell, taste and touch of diverse cultures. My senses are on alert, everything is more vivid. As an outsider I become an observer and absorber. What I see and experience fires my writing.

I am magnetically drawn towards the East, to Africa and to all those far-flung places I have as yet only finger-travelled on maps or visited through books. Looking at Great Britain on an accurate* world map, one sees how very small this country is. There is a huge world out there to explore, learn from and most importantly for me, to place an understanding of my race within a world-wide framework.

Europe's empires have disappeared in name but no matter how far away from Europe I travel, the lingering taste of colonialism is always omnipresent. Yet I am British and as such I too have reaped the rewards of the colonial legacy. For example, I had a commendable school education and when I visit children in other parts of the world who are really desperate to study but have no pens, paper or books, then I am made acutely aware that I have had everything I needed with which to pursue a formal education or to educate myself. This awareness is a driving impetus for putting my pen to my paper and getting on with it!

Some of the poetry in this book was born out of my various journeys.

The poem THE GIRL WHO KEPT ON STARING is directly based on one experience of Madagascar; an isolated island off the East African coast which was a French colony until 1960. The island really is beautiful but how can I enjoy the beauty when faced with the poverty? Time and again I question the role of the tourist in so-called Third World countries. It is easy to see the word 'tourist' as synonymous with the word 'exploitation'; relatively rich foreigners utilizing the resources of poor countries for a fraction of the cost that they would pay at home. Also, behaving abominably, to boot. Frequently falling into the Me - Master / You - Slave syndrome (if they can get away with it). I once witnessed a tourist haggle over a twenty pence cab fare when the same trip would have cost him at least ten pounds here in England. It does have to be said, however, that the tourist trade does bring in some much needed income. Who gets it and who does not is another matter again.

Madagascar is one of the poorest countries in the world. This poverty is highly visible but not, apparently, to the growing numbers of French and German tourists who holiday there. To hear cardboard shacks described as 'quaint' and to see the way in which the beggars in the capital Antananarivo are scorned is shocking. Another time I saw a tourist offer a beggar some money. Each time the beggar moved forward to take the money, the tourist withdrew his hand and enjoyed this joke with his pals. This continued, *ad nauseam*, until he finally threw a single coin onto the ground and left.

In 1986 I visited Egypt. We had booked into a very large old colonial hotel in Luxor which had obviously once been exceedingly grand but which was now very musty and decrepit. Except for a handful of other guests the hotel was empty. It reminded me of the way in which I like to visit museums and old monuments. With no distraction it is possible to experience an uninterrupted contact between myself and the objects I have come to see. That time-worn hotel was full of the geist of the European Society who once strolled down the lush corridors and danced out on the verandah under a star-spangled African sky. I could make out the Egyptian waiters who were standing to attention in the background. Invisible, except when called upon to service a guest.

But I was overjoyed to be in Egypt which I found to be the most historically fascinating and inspiring country I had ever visited. I was overawed to sit by the great River Nile itself which is often used as a symbol of African blood coursing through the ages. An image of power, renewal, timelessness. I did not know then that the ancient Greeks whom we have been taught were the parents of our modern Western civilization were in truth the children of the ancient Egyptians who in turn were the offspring of the Ethiopian civilization. This little snippet of information has been deliberately withheld from us and buried under the notable achievements of the Western world. Thankfully, some historians are putting the record straight and we are hearing about all the other great African nations and civilizations which have been omitted from history books.

The Coloniser and Slaver records history to suit himself. The truths which do not fit into his scheme of things are either re-arranged to glorify himself or simply removed. During the past five hundred years he has invented derogatory concepts of Africans to justify his inhuman and unforgivable actions in Africa. Later, he cannot separate truth from his fiction and except for those who know better, he believes in his own made-to-measure mythology. We pay the price today - all over the African diaspora and in the continent itself.

74

One night I went out onto the balcony of my room and looked out onto the Nile which ran quietly before me. I wrote SIMPLE SCRIBE.

As a people our sense of self is injured by a lack of knowledge of our vast and rich heritage - the soil out of which we have grown. On one level the poem THE ORATOR attempts to resurrect the memory of some of our ancient leaders. We begin by naming our ancestors. Calling their names out into the air for the wind to carry them around the earth. As a woman my foremothers come first but still today there are those whose only interest is to recall the world according to Man and her stories are kept underground or marginalised. Surely this is assuming the same mantle as the coloniser?

A similar herstorical theme runs through the poem ANTIQUE GOLD AND BURNING ROSE. As Black people born in Europe we have been inundated and overwhelmed with almost exclusively White images of achievement. *En masse*, these serve to belittle us. Now we are digging deeper into our past and finding the people and the stories which will serve to strengthen our belief in ourselves and our capabilities.

I wrote ANTIQUE GOLD AND BURNING ROSE in Spain, where, due to its close proximity to Britain, I have spent a considerable amount of time. Most people will consider Spain to be an Hispanic country with a corresponding heritage. Nothing could be further from the truth. For eight hundred years, up until the thirteenth century, the Spaniards were conquered and ruled by the African Moorish Empire. Spain was transformed from a backward and uncultured country into an unrivalled centre for the arts and sciences. When the Moors left, so too did the civilization they had created. Spain has never recovered its former glory.

Sometimes I have an attraction for a country. There is something about the people, the landscape, the way of life. I may not understand why a particular place appeals to me but if I stop and think about how both ancient and modern Africans have travelled this globe, since time immemorial, and left their imprints nearly everywhere, then I understand more.

The name Zenobia belonged to a legendary Black queen and warrior of the East who died circa A.D. 272. Her enormous empire, Palmyra, extended the land we now know as Iraq through to Southern Africa. She was as famous as Cleopatra and indeed she conquered Egypt which she added to her empire. Zenobia was also the first name of my paternal grandmother who lived and died in Nigeria and whom I never met.

75

I wrote the Poem ZENOBIA whilst staying on the Greek island of Crete. Like Spain, Crete is also imbued with a resonant African past. One set of early inhabitants of Crete were the Minoans who came from, amongst other places - Africa. (Another snippet of information usually excluded from tourist brochures). The southern coast of Crete fringes the Libyan Sea, so this is hardly surprising. So was it very surprising that I picked up on the African presence moving around the island? Or did it pick me up!

One summer night I was camping by the coast and on the flat of a cliff. A sirocco blew in from North Africa. I had never experienced such a wind force before. It was hot, dusty, strong, strange, frightening and it raged in from the sea for hours. By the time it had subsided it had left quite a lot of destruction in it's wake. It seemed a poignant symbol at the time. I could just imagine how the winds would have brought the African seamen to the island in the old days. The following morning was beautifully sunny and a calm lay over the island.

I believe in the power of the pen. So too did the Egyptians, Moors and other African nations who had great libraries. The Egyptians possessed the greatest library in the world where they had accumulated masses of knowledge about the ancient world. This library was deliberately destroyed by Christians in A.D. 389. Other African libraries were also destroyed by invading armies. What an immeasurable loss! What information those weighty tomes would have revealed to us.

I find that there is no set rule for the creation of a poem, it will evolve and usually takes on a life of its own. Later I use my outside eye to make sense of what I have written. Then comes the hardest part of innumerable re-writes. As a poet I can but present images of my own perceptions. You may, in this instance, use my camera, but always you look through your own lens; wide-angle?, single-lens?, telephoto?, mirror-lens?

Although my writing is influenced by my travels this does not mean that I always write directly about the places I visit. All passages are inter-linked. To travel is to follow the chains, discover where they have come from, where they branch out, break, seek the missing links and dream the day they are complete.

Our elders and ancestors have laid the foundations for our living today as we are preparing the ground for future generations.

AUTUMN 1990
LONDON

* Peter's Projection Map

76

ZENOBIA

Zenobia wore a crown
of thinly sliced shaped ivory leaves.
A delicate twist of each one,
forming a magical halo -
Light Of Life,
the summer that she came to us.

Our parched cracked lips
trembled in anticipation.
Young thirsty eyes devoured
the bevy of jewels cascading
along the seams and ridges
of her roundsome frame.

'Your obedient servants' we gasped,
'Melon seeds, Turquoise, Rubies, Amethysts.'
Florid words fell like unwanted cherry pips,
now to lie and bleach on stone.

Our thin dry bodies knelt in homage
as Zenobia strode towards us
from the foothills.

Finely coiled hennaed hair
dancing about her thighs.

Clenched teeth of cowrie shells
draped from her noble neck.

Swan vision in ebony rising before us,
each movement a serenade.

Limbs a symphony in ancient mountain ranges.
Shells transformed to golden sun pearls.

Her laughter sweeping across savannahs,
singing from rock to water,
rebounding in caverns,
gushing into dells,
melting our hardness,
washing our tiredness away.

(She had come to us when our heads-
helmets of molten lead, throbbed in hope
for some last recognition)

Zenobia was as large as we were diminished.
As alive as we were dying.

77

Placed rosaries of wild hibiscus
on our fragile points.
Rubbed our souls for soothing:
tip tongued slurring for sure
over ripe watermelons.
Each pip a seed, each seed a growth,
each growth - life.

Zenobia, as stolid
as an old and mighty warrior.
Designs of scars, battle marked patches,
as smooth as sea washed pebbles - shocking!

From high noon to sundown
we blazed and buzzed like hot island bees
on sweet cherry trees.
Swimming in the cooling of aqua sources.
Playing upon thick soft mats
of brum and floribunda.
Trying to live again
before late afternoon in the heat.

But Zenobia came and left
before the sun had set,
before our sweat had dried
to hard nodules or nothingness,
before the flowers
had withered and shrivelled,
before she would age with us,
before she would die with us.

Her regents stride back to the foothills;
a sheen of polished mahogany,
escaping between jagged and shearing rock
as quickly as she had entered.

Daylight transferred to sea to night,
and Zenobia - carefully wrapped and placed
in our storehouse of memories -
    - that summer.

1987

THE ORATOR

The Orator mouthspeaks the traditions
that we call upon.
What he has omitted through practice,
no longer with forethought,
no longer with malice;
is what we need to hear.

The Orator's words contain a legacy -
a wave re-doubling
and sweeping over centuries.
Older than the Book,
now dog-eared leaves.
A convincing book for most is there.

Unlike the Orator
who stands upon the Golden Stool;
a sign of the time, the tribe, the land.
Brandishing the brush or the stick.
(Yes! Him Big Doctor Stick!)

Speaking forth his stories
in accordance with the custom
for our ears sealed with moss;
listening lowly at the point
where the cloud covets the sun -
in the shadow.

The Orator has told his sons
of the Mau Mau's of Kenya,
Toussaint of Haiti, Shaka of Azania.
Of the land, of the blood
when North enters South;
East meets West.

For the boy child's initiation rite,
with one majestic flourish of the arm
he speaks "This is all you need to know
of the heritage, the life -
the root of these times."

A message travels through the earth,
the air promising a tornado;
winds filter through walls - out forests
plays music on the dust;
whispers calling the orator to heel
on the rise and fall of the soil.

Voices so faint few can hear
call through countries, continents, nations.
Bush-Talk, Home-Talk takes hold of the root
sits a ring to induce our beginning
beyond the fluidity of the Orator's speech.

The passage is clear, untraced for years.
Led by Queen Nzinga of Angola,
Amina of Hausaland, Hatshepsut
of Old Egypt - breathe through
a sarcophagus of stone as the whisper
evokes the dead - the Silenced.

The Orator stands -
brown leathered feet to the ground.
A Power. A Force. A Weight.
Deaf to the rumbling surging underfoot,
inner soil in movements upwards.

With a wave and a flourish
the Orator fires passion
as the lines of his tales are re-told,
omitting those words sewn out of his story
that gain strength as they stir underground.
For the murmur transmutes to a heave
and a push to stay the Orator's hand.

The Orator's mouth speaks the traditions
that we call upon.
But what he has omitted through deed,
through practice, is the sound
of our legacy as it stirs
through our lands.

1986

NATIONAL MEMORIES

Patience the storyteller,
a plain quiet woman,
eyes translucent crystals:
steady,   alert,
took my hand,   led me
to a tree in full bloom;
softly fluffed petals
blurring a-windy skyscape,
sat me down beside her.
I asked her to begin:

80

"I am a quiet woman.
My silence is rooted in my spine,
each vertebrae a rock nugget,
no longer malleable but hard
within this confine of fleshmuscle.

I am elder to the dispossessed.
My eyes, clear crystal reflectors
are rare - sharply I watch
the tillers and reapers;
the bulge of coin filled pockets.

I am mother of Africa's diaspora.
My children are lonely.
Wander Western galleries for a painting
that reflects their precise images,
some learning to paint their own.

My nose is Arawak -
Island bay rebels -
a pure line. I know I will not live long
but survive through my descendants.
I cannot afford to die.

My cheekbones - finely sculptured wood.
Many scars sweeping both
where I was slashed to tell my age.
They could not tell
for I live beyond their years.

My lips - torn leather.
Ragged from biting to stop speaking
for I knew not how then
and had to learn through pain.
The swelling subsided, gradually.

My tongue - Aboriginal
Sliced by a deadly serrated knife.
So I speak in two tongues,
study the plains in rebellion.
I have been betrayed.

My chin is soft but not weak.
Inherited from the shifting
sand dunes of the desert,
that disperses often
but will always move as one.

My breasts are bitter women
who loved but did not receive,
whose milk gives life to millions,
who cross the earth in anger
long after death.

My liver is Maori
and the knowledge of earth's cycles.
If Pakeha leaves
the healing sea and land
again will come into its own.

My heart is the soul of Africa:
tired, old, pensive.
Nurturing its own,
re-building fortresses;
alive and well in struggle - Africa.

My arms were bound in India.
Cross blindly held
and burning on a pyre.
My charred remains will return
to haunt those who led me there.

My calves - carved
the divinities of all Nation Peoples
that watch the earth come
full circle in justice;
preparing your nightmare.

My ankles were passing ships.
I'm glad that they passed with no bounty
for that was our saving,
They were 'lost at sea',
but we 'undiscovered', lived longer.

My feet are the hooves of warriors,
riding the land by right -
who no one remembers,
history forgot,
women who fought to the last.

O, but I am a quiet woman.
Eyes like cut crystal reflectors.
Carrying the past on my tongue
like the sting of a wasp.
Knowing the sequence of man's slaughters.

Patience the storyteller, stopped
as abruptly as the screeching
brakes of a car.
I had heard her and would be forever thankful.
The tree was no longer in full bloom
for tempests had robbed it
to a dark prepared outline
against a deceptively calm sky.

(Sometime later I remembered
and wondered about crystal, cycles,
and a plain quiet woman
with land rites on her mind,
passion in her heart,
and a fierceness made of rock;
the root of nations.)

1988

SEABODYWOMAN

Lover,
your sea laughter awakens
my body as the waters gaily splash
and swimming love within my spirit.
The rays of the sun
have deepened your browness,
your full strong shape sways
to the ebony keys as the wild hairs
around your belly glisten
soft and tough and black as jet,
travelling towards the forest
that is your heart,
protecting and warming
our source.

Your body
rich, smooth and plush velvet.
Shaped to be held,
held to be loved
as the cool sea breeze
washes away our fears,
cools our heat.
Hey! Lets get up and walk
barefoot and nappy headed
African princesses strolling
along the ivory coast,
heads held high and feeling
the sun beat upon the purple-red
that is our backs
as the wind caresses our bodies
our inner thighs
meet and part
meet and part
meet and part

Lover,
your eyes have become
accustomed to the sea in them
not needing to focus
or turn away
as our warm brown bodies
drip droplets of cool sealets
upon this newly dawning singing continent
of a ...Whoopla!
          Whoopla!
               Whoopla!

I blow
a long hot whisper of air
on your brow
...Lover...

1984

ANTIQUE GOLD AND BURNING ROSE

My memory has been chased
across a trimly cut lawn;
snatched by a fist of wind
and flung beyond the rim
of the defined horizon.

My thoughts defy the logical
sequence of order, but not
always the debris   so
sweep it all away:
dead leaves   weeds   thorns
small rocks   stones   twigs
until the soil breathes
ready for memory to return.

II

Once I found you on a plane
bound for the Sudan.

Your long chiseled profile
proudly directed ahead;

skillfully plaited hair
wrought like fine silver filigree;

tall regal body sweeping along the aisle
to the swish of silky pink robes
flowing from blue-black skin;

Sandalwood seducing the anonymous air
as you floated - passing.

I, inhaling your perfume
and merrily merrily drowning.

Egypt saw you wrapped in black,
two slits for naked eyes:

dark calm ponds
heightened by water lilies,
graced by weeping willow lashes -
pale long necked ferns - all
glistening in a dewy light.

                    not one word we spared each other
                    not one word fell in contact
                    of any spoken language

III

At night I hover on the periphery,
disjointed edges of dreaming,
travelling across the divide.
Remembering the years are falling
apart like sad autumn leaves.
I will journey before my lifetime,
race to the waiting hub
of my subconscious circle;
greet and clasp in sisterly
blood-finger-knots.

I recall Cleopatra who drank
the alien juice of the downfall.
Dido Elizabeth Lindsay, poised
in a portrait of 18th century England.
Mary Seacole, heroic nurse of the Crimea,
obliterated from his story books since;
two toasts of swinging Europe,
Bricktop in Rome, Baker in Paris.
One ran the top nightclub,
the other performed in them.
Nanny of the Marroons,
leader against slavery in Jamaica.

Names, faces, memories.
I churn them over and over
like cement in a mixer
until they are solid foundation.
Strong. Lasting. Remembered.

            Forever and a day - the namesakes
            Antique Gold and Burning Rose

for age, richness, the fire and the beauty.

1988

THE GIRL WHO KEPT ON STARING

This roaring land's beauty
beset by constant poverty;
silently pleading children's cases
which tourist-time usually turns
into obscure or forgotten passages.
Only this time I live
with the testing visual memory
of a slow moving reel
of Tanarivo * beggary
at the Cafe Colbert -
my last day on the island.

I gave money to some
and the others followed me
until my walk was mobbed
by the desperate, the hungry
encircling me, begging
for more coins for food
for the babies who have learnt
to cry at a mother's command.
Little boys pull funny faces for me
so that amused I'd give more and more
until reaching the upper Town,
hemmed in on all four sides
so that I could not step or turn
beyond the crowd's wishes,
they then quickly dispersed
or were shooed away by porters,
leaving me to walk unhindered
to a seat outside.

"Ils ont trés riche. Donnez pas votre argent,"
said the corpulent, decadent-lipped
pink Frenchman at my table.
"Ils ne sont pas pauvres, seulement paraisseux."
Dragon puffing whisky/Marlboro fumes
into my stone astonished face.

Watching the teenage paper sellers
dash up and down the road
thrusting Le Midi at irked adults
who at every step are stopped
by one seller or another.
Red frocked porters chasing
beggars away (half-heartedly)
whilst the pale arm of wealth
dipped thick gold bracelets
into a waiting Mercedes Benz,
dangled crisp banknotes at doormen

for their prompt smiling service.
And then - amid the flurry
of tall white-hatted waiters
gliding in quick succession.
One elegantly raised hand
bearing stacked white boxes
of sumptuous cream gateaux
to the Patisserie Colbert
next door - I saw you two
standing still across the busy way.
For how long I do not know
but now surely transfixed on me;
your silently pleading children's faces.

Sister and brother I think you were,
no matter it made no difference
as I carefully turned away
only to unwillingly return my eyes
through the powerful medium
of your silent calling, and the sight
of two boney outstretched hands:
… unmoving … unyielding…
waiting for hard round coins
to be placed in the soft
of young brown palms.

Eyes of the older child
did not move from me.
Blatant with resentment.
Infused in pain, hurt
and Oh the touch of hate
in so young a girl!
I wished you would stop staring.
Turn away from me. Please!
Oh! child!
Stop this terrible confrontation.
This nightmare
where the rough textured underbelly
of your poverty
challenges my Western lifestyle.
I wanted you to stop staring.
to turn away.
For I, a Black face
in this merry montage of White ones.
Quiet amid a loud sound reel
of joie de vivre, chatter, clatter,
mellifluous-sexed vowels -
all - smouldering in the hazy smoke
of Gitanes and Gauloise,
am for you - the accessible target.
Of course. Yet I,

seated in their mock Parisian café
am not one of them
Indeed this battalion actively
against our family interest.
But how can I say I'm of your family
when my coins represent
a 'gold-paved' world away in Europe.

There is only you and I here.
You - firing bullets
into my browned-off head
until I rise
giving you what you ask for.
(Knowing it is not
or will ever be enough.)

Then it starts all over again.
Your eyes. Your pleading. Pain. The Silence.
Slicing through the kefuffle
of street activity.

Unswerving eyes
shooting through passing Peugeots.

Fixed grip
unmoved by the high heels of glamour women.

Tree-like rootedness
before annoyed arm waving porters.

Biblical, deadpan hands
crying 'Give more. Give more'.
As articulate as Marceau.
Thin as a reed.

Expertly aiming
at the heart of my consciousness
for this is your daily battleground
for food: an income for survival.

This I call tableaux
of unrelenting poverty
set against a backdrop
of this island's raging beauty.

* Antananarivo - capital of Madagascar

1988

SIMPLE SCRIBE

I am a simple scribe
looking out at the night Nile,
surveying the lights
dabbling on the banks
where the Bedouins stay.

I am a simple scribe
capturing the colours of this land,
aligning my paper
to learn the dimensions.

I am a simple scribe
remembering the trade of the people,
connecting the history
to our present lives.

I am a simple scribe
listening to the night life:
carriages and motors
rattle their way by.

I am a simple scribe
calling upon the forces
asking for some guidance,
some better way.

I am a simple scribe
trying to learn so that I can pass on.
Trying to listen so that I can hear.
Trying to move so that I can enter.

1986

Maud Sulter

Zabat: **Poetics of a Family Tree** – Extracts

FIRE

CADENCES

Cadences flare
black night
alludes
to untold
tales from
the darkness.

Fingers rake
the debris
of the past
demanding
recognition
of the Self.

Mirrored
visions
here
fragments
regain
wholeness.

Magic
sets
the
fire
aflame
we go.

Phoenix come rise
from the flame
through gold light
to orange fire
sparked smoke
darting wayward.

Reclaiming
that which was
ours which is now
ours again.

Unknown words
dance like
mirambas
across
the space
and time
between us.

We become one.

As warriors
we stalk
this night

the fierce
fired red
head
of the knife
incises
our palms
we clench
a fist
and become
each
the other

fearlessly.

Blood
mingles
with
sweat
and
our tears.

Unity transfixes us
and we hang
suspended
in this European
time and space
but travel
centuries
to our
birthright.

RITES OF PASSAGE

Cowries
scattered
at the
leather
thonged
feet of
the young
woman

promising
fertility.

The belly swells
moonly blood
comes seeds
fall to
the wind
each month
replaced
by another
patiently

the Seer
waits.

Time cannot be hampered
by the distorted
cycle of the West
time cannot be harnessed.

Come see
my hair
plaits
adorn
my
head
each
in
turn
adorned
with shells.

Captivating
all who hear
and see the bounty.

Come hear
my lips sing
sweet mysteries.

A young woman
I wait
sometimes
angry
sometimes
calm

my own
initiation
rite awaits.

Here in a land of no sun I await the break of day

Out there somewhere you wait for me
in another country
place and time

You see I

And know that the time will come
for us to be
re-united.

I not knowing this feel a growing frustration
and cut off the crown
which was my glory

My power fades.   I grow weak
My skin pales
as putrified
my mind spews
in pornographic
clichés.   My body rebels
against me.

Bent double   back   Bent   forward   under
Images repel yet excite me

Nothing and no-one comes to my inner sanctum
I alone listen to the beating
of my heart
as my spirit
soars away from me.

Screaming
I chase it
near naked
along an urban
highway

lorry drivers
leer and masturbate

their semen poisons all it touches

I run
I run
I run

for miles
each day

I run

my body sweats
the muscles
no longer
rebel knowing
that this is my
only hope of survival.

Stay alive   Stay alive   Stay alive

For the sake of our future.   Stay alive.
Home again
the sweat
cools.

I run my hand
between my honey
brown thighs
but still
feel nothing
except an empty
vacant pulse

it mocks
by chanting
Ka
Ka
Ka

I know not
what it means
   Ka
   Ka
   Ka

Know not
what
it means.

BY THE POND

By the pond
I await
a swansong.

Alone
I hear
the dull
thud of cricket
ball on willow.

Comforted
I see the ball
sweep the groove
of their groin
seductively.

Fearing the welling there
yet I lust
after the knife
edge pleat of the cream
flannels crease incised
sharp as a surgeons
scalpel.

They do not even see me
but I know their power
                their threat.

Crouched behind the hedge
I long for something
which I have
never had.

Nothing comes of this longing
                        but more longing.

Feast
eat
greedily
at my limbs

Ragged

Depraved

An object
you consume

I understand
the threat
of the man
in the close
who bear hugs
me almost to
submission
rubs me
rythmically
against him

His flacid penis
hardens his eyes
grow colder

Longing to flee I kick   I kick
yet make no sound

He lets me go   –   fearfully
His mind considers   –   possibilities

Strangle her.   Fingers tight
around the throat.   Rape
the life out
of her
orally
anally
vaginally.   Take
the socially constructed
virginity and make
out of it a corpse.

' Hide the body in the coal bunker

No one would find it for days
and who would miss a little
coloured girl.

       And who
       would
       miss
       a
       little
       coloured
       girl.

And who would miss a little
coloured girl   –   Here?

AFRICA BECKONS

SALINE DIAMONDS

Between the movements of the ticking clock
the baby moved. like a flutter of gossamer
light as helium. mighty as ten thousand
butterflies. at the moment of conception
she had been there. in spirit attuned

bearing witness to the new life sparked
like a firefly in the depths of a Cuban
night. at the core of her being her body
began its flight. two saline diamonds welled
then softly slid onto already swelling breasts

MEMORIES

SHORT STORY

The
blue
well of
wishing

sinking into
dark berry
sheets
her skin
charged
by the cool
cotton weave

an ecstatic sigh
emissed from
her lips
jarred
the silence
of the room

the air was
electric as
the
storm
approached.

EARTH

BOUNTY

Tulips spilled sensuous stamen
scattering intense purple
pigment across glass topped table.

Blown petals sunkissed yellow
shot through with spiced pink
flanked full and open cores.

Had Nature been in attendance
to her full omnipotence fat
bumble bees would hover
patiently collecting nectar
for the Goddess. Backleg pouches
overflowing as returning posses
deliver up their tributes.

Alas our Sister slept too deep
this May afternoon. No platoon
in striped regalia came creeping
to collect Her bounty. And so
she also neglected to attend
our twentieth century fable.

HISTORICAL OBJECTS

Cave drawings 1715k years old
humanities oldest representation
of our form Blackwoman her soul
sits uneasy in a Viennese prison.
Egyptian mummified bodies stolen
rot uneasily in European hells
of culture. So sets the scene
of us Blackwomen in Europe.
We read pornographic versions
of African Jeanne Duval as muse
destroyed by Baudelairean pox
les fleurs du mal black venus.

Slavery days. And here I find
you still on the planation now
differently guised yet still
a bondage. And Freedom freedom
has an empty call when I see you
still chained to their supremacist
belief in themselves. They cannot
be allowed any longer to rewrite
our experience; call it marxist
or feminist, history or herstory
no-longer no more. Ka is rising.
Ka is rising. Listen. Listen
you can hear her call. For Ka
is rising. Ka is rising. Hear
come hear her call.

FULL CYCLE

From somewhere over the Isle of Cloves
the Watcher rises from the stool and chants
an incantation. The air hung heavy with the
scents of sweet smelling plants – lemon grass
jasmine a spiced edge of cinnamon and mace.

The Ka is risen.

MaShulan who cursed Livingstone. That trip
was his last. Damned his house. We must make
it no more than ashes. Bring the tower to the
ground. And we shall not mourn its passing
when still from Tanzania to Scotland the child
learns of his *good christian* intent. Mud huts
they show as proof of their *civilisation*. Over
our infinite cultures. Civilisation can never
be written in the blood and bones of slavery.

Daughters she cries
learn the tongues
of this worlds voices
teach the children

of their wonder
love as only a woman can
take up the pen, the brush,
explosive, gun
and name
yes name
yourself
black
woman
zami
proud
name yourself
never forget
our herstory.

Whatever fragment you find
preserve
recognise
your self
      heritage
      responsibility
      worth
more
precious
than
gold
weights.

The Spirit of Ka.

BLACKWOMANSONG

DELETE AND ENTER

Hey Brother. Nice seeing ya.
Travelling the contours of that
cragged not quite ebony face
through its valleys
now of death but still fine fine.

Journeying with you Griot
of our urban experience
voice rasps fingers gesture
from mere english futures are carved.

Our eyes met across a sea of black
and I foolish-like casually say
to myself Hey Brother. Nice seeing ya.
Promise to write you but the pen never
meets paper. I talk to you in my head.
Long distance. Sempiternal communication.
Walk with you. Hear the fury of Fire Next Time
sufferation plague pestilence starvation terrors
not of our making multinationals raping and
the cold war does not thaw though they
would like us to believe it. Hell
one Man believes in Armageddon
and does the other guy know God?

We ain't angry man we're mad
some mad bad niggers that's us
                'delete and enter if you must
                    a more contemporary definition...
And yeah, There Be Dragons when and where
black faggotry and dykedom meet
                'delete and enter if you must
                    a more contemporary definition...
coz time passes and skipping bullets diseases
poverty hate is real-life here. No one can be sure
to be here to see to the finer points of language
linguistics or typesetting errors – though I know we
call ourselves Black and I undoubtedly name myself Zami.

Our call and response wakes the world
voice no longer silent from fear but hungry
with passion. You make me Jimmy. You make me.

Ko na bra. Exile
is not a voluntary leaving.
We do not choose our birthing
nor perhaps our death but to die
knowing you loved me like you loved
the world hot hot as chilli-pepper
is a beter way of living to the end.

You make me James Baldwin, you make me
and I will still cry biter tears
feel my body disobey the command
to be brave. For true strength is all,
weakness a cold endless death.
And us? We will live forever at the tip
of each others vocabularies
at the edge of the Africa we know.
Fly back Jimmy. Fly back and wait
at the mountain top where family will
meet again someday; the Brethren and
the Sistren, to decide the naming
of the Sun. In our own tongue.

These extracts are taken from   *Zabat: Poetics of a Family Tree*
                                 Urban Fox Press 1989
                                 ISBN 1 872124 05 4

Also by Maud Sulter   AS A BLACKWOMAN
                                 (Akira Press 1985)
                                 Urban Fox Press 1989
                                 ISBN 872124 00 3

Publicity shot, Delta Streete, "IN THE DEEP" (1990)
photo credit M. Sulter

Delta Streete

In The Deep: A feminine reclamation of self

In The Deep developed as a response to the linear recitation of history in terms of modernism, modern art and modernity. (A brief presented to me by the commissioning organisation The Elbow Room.) This broad history was connected to my knowledge that Blackwomen create and have always created art. It is a knowledge that counteracts the popular assumption that their presence is of little or no significance to historical developments. This of course is not the case. Blackwomen's creative development has, as with most Black artistic practice, greatly influenced the creative progression of the arts. But the contribution of Black peoples has either been assimilated into the historical progression of western history or been undermined. *In The Deep* is a piece which acknowledges this process and talks of the psychological oppression used to undermine and dismiss Blackwomen's experiences. At the same time it explored how their survival becomes linked with day to day living. The piece comes from my need to understand ways of connecting with this experience rather than emphasising the purpose of oppression, which is self evident.

In The Deep travels along the levels at which Blackwomen encounter and positively connect with life. It operates from an understanding of these experiences in sexual as well as racial terms. For I recognise the need to negotiate ways through these principles which are common to all Blackwomen, however different they may be. The issues of race, sexuality and gender have an immediate impact on the lives of women of the Black diaspora including their creative selves. However, these principles are ordered by imperialist pursuits and patriarchal societal values which deny and prevent the widespread dissemination of work produced by Blackwomen.

There has, until recent history, been very little dialogue relating to art by Blackwomen. The denial of this presence clearly does not mean the work has not been made. It does however show how little equipped male supremacy is to deal with the profound subtleties inherent in this female experience. It is generally understood that a work of art's authority to represent the world is not held in its uniqueness but is based on the idea of a universal modern aesthetic – modernism in this case. (Until recent times interpretation of this concept was the privilege of white male supremacy.) It was a vision that used certain forms and developments of form to present and represent itself in different areas. As David Dorsey explains in an essay entitled *The Art of Mari Evans* (p.170, Black Women Writers, ed. Mari Evans, Pluto edition 1985).

> *There are no universal formal criteria in literature, as there are no universal formal scales in music. Even our reaction to new forms is based on their relation to familiar structures. To say that the shapes of beauty are established by cultures implies that the shapes of beauty embraced by Afro-Americans are not the same as those of Euro-Americans. But the formal canons of Euro-American – that is European-literature are among the most codified in human history. Ever since Aristotle they have been subject to intensive description and analysis. Furthermore, even without the incentive of colonialism they have been perceived as 'universal' principles which characterise art itself, rather than the art of one atypical group of related cultures.*

The art which these artistic values or 'principles' as Dorsey describes them, is based on its content. This is due to historical evolutions in ideas about taste and forms. As this 'universal' concept of art developed the artistic values frequently presented, was a male vision which dominated the power systems that make valid certain artistic representation. The effect is a simultaneous negation of others.

Because of this it has often been thought that to make self representations meant making art centred firmly in the male vision of masculinity. The problem with this assumption is that it confirms the white masculine perspective as the only valid human experience. This constant confirmation has led to the development of art that places woman's femininity as passive objects given the role of representating what, for men is unpresentable. The role of femininity can, in this way, be seen as a state of false representation, a simulation of the unreal, a seduction. These crude definitions of women's femininity have been broken down due to the development of feminist analysis on society as well as the growing value placed by Blackpeople on their cultural experiences. These are changes which voice the ever present need for perceptive, not hostile, analysis of art made by people outside the white male vision.

In The Deep explores Blackwomen's femininity beyond this masculine vision, working to create artistic expression centred around Blackwoman's experiences. The piece works on the premise that the analytical stripping of white masculine arts vision allows Blackwomen to reclaim the lost terrain of their creativity. The need for the constant reclamation of Black artistic tradition is paramount in this climate where these traditions once protected by our ancestors, require open and conscious development.

108

OLUSOLA
OYELEYE

In Music's Tattered Hand I Lay My Heart

A SHORT OVERVIEW OF WORKING IN OPERA AT ENO

ACT I

"In music's tattered hand I lay my heart..."

Many people may say that Opera is an elitist art form, particularly when tracing its European origins to the Court music of the Renaissance. Perhaps if the European vision was not so obtuse, then people might wish to discover that in many cultures there is a form of opera - an oral story-telling that far outdates its European counterpart. In the Yoruba culture one such tradition is rárà chanted by men and women, old or young, for entertainment on social occasions. Ìjálá is performed by hunters or devotees of Ogun, the Yorùbá divinity of iron. Èsà is chanted by masque ürades, while ekún ìyawó is sung by brides on the eve of their marriage. Each of these forms has its own characteristic musical style. Close examination will make it evidently clear that there is a connection. So it is not a real surprise to me that I should want to work in this medium, the biggest problem would be access, which of course relies heavily on other peoples perceptions.

In 1987 I was selected from 400 applicants to take part in the first BP Young Directors Festival at Battersea Arts Centre in London - on the basis of my CV, a three hour workshop and my response to two questions, which I share with you now:

WHY I WANT TO DIRECT

As a black person born and brought up in Britain, I see very little within our theatre that reflects my experience. Where I am represented, rather than being positively researched, characterisations and presentations are based on obtuse assumptions. For example an actor is required to have an 'african' / 'west indian' accent, no definition, whereas we would not ask for an accent from 'up north somewhere'. As theatre, in my opinion, has to be mentally challenging, and visually stimulating, I want to be part of a change that recognises with sensitivity and social awareness, the importance of developing a strong communication between topic, performance and audience. This invariably dictates what I would choose to direct. My interest lies solely in developing new writing and while I have acquired extensive knowledge of several forms, I use that knowledge to look forward.

WHAT I FEEL DIRECTING IS

To me directing is not simply a career choice, it is a vocation. A director is, at best, a catalyst responsible for initiating and guiding a chain of reactions, yet is able to come out 'unchanged' to allow the process to grow, creating an atmosphere where performance is not 'just learning lines for the next job'. The relationship between the writer, the performers and the production team, is vital in terms of the development of mutual respect. It is important to have experience of as many aspects of production as possible in order to facilitate the exchange of knowledge. Directing needs to challenge , stimulate, question and yet maintain the responsibility of entertainment. A director may 'see' the 'whole', but if the 'soul' does not come from within the process it will always remain superficial. Although it can at times be tremendously frustrating, being part of the creative process means sowing a seed and allowing it, with guidance, the space to grow.

I rediscovered these paragraphs and they became a personal guideline. I do feel the need to continually reassess the well of my motivation. Like many people I could hum along with several opera songs, but I did not necessarily know from which operas they came. I was inspired by singers: Marian Anderson, Paul Robeson, more recently Shirley Verrett, - particularly her role as L'Africaine, Grace Bumbry, Jessye Norman and Wilhemina Fernandez. I knew no particular directors and in general I found the medium quite dry until I started working in it.

It was important for me to have the opportunity to work in a large house with extensive facilities. To develop ones creative skills we must have access to as many differing experiences as possible. I cannot say what the opportunities for blackwomen and blackmen in the area are. The reaction of my peers ranged from euphoria to ambivalence. What was I trying to achieve by working in this medium? I felt very strongly that I was giving myself the opportunity to work with a large budget, where there were still a lot of mysteries to unfold and I feel I get that experience at English National Opera (ENO).

I first worked with ENO in 1987 co-ordinating their Youth Opera festival at the Young Vic. Although I enjoy administration, I was beginning to feel like Jacqueline of all trades and mistress of many. I felt my energies were too dispersed and I wanted to concentrate on writing and directing. On the strength of this work I was offered one production, the opportunity of working as staff producer on *The Mikado*. Then the Baylis programme approached the Arts Council for a training bursary and two years later I became ENO's first Arts Council Trainee Producer.

I worked on five productions. A new youth opera on ecology called *A SMALL GREEN SPACE*, which had a national tour including a trip to Barrow-in-Furness - home of a nuclear power station. I did ask if the insurance covered individual contamination from nuclear pollutants! Besides assisting the producer, I was responsible for rehearsing each new chorus and the small parts. *KATYA KABANOVA*, a 20th century opera by the Czech composer Jánacek followed, then an early opera *THE RETURN OF ULYSSES*, by Monteverdi. The instrumentation was so sparse that you could hear every word the singers sang. *BEATRICE ET BENEDICT* after Shakespeare, then *THE MIKADO* for a second time.

Responsibilities include cover rehearsals, getting the show on stage and maintainence of the production. Tact, diplomacy and patience are always good virtues to have at hand.

ACT 2

"A song whose melody echoed so piercingly that birds wept."

There is a wonderful sense of achievement when you move into a new genre. However, ones feet should never float too high from the ground. Once, on coming into the Coliseum, I was asked at the front desk by the new receptionist, if I was coming for an interview for a job in the canteen. I talked to the catering staff a lot and it is a real pity that there is no connection with the main house, not even for dress rehearsals. There was a limited amount of feedback and there were times that I felt I was trying to gauge myself in a vacuum. At the end of the day I was aware that I had to work from the inside out and the outside in at the same time. Trying to use my creative abilities, while maintaining my dignity. I made a point of talking about Nigerian culture because I felt it was important to remind people that I am part of a long tradition and not a so called 'Black British' - a term that I feel is a non-entity description which dismisses my

111

culture and over 400 years of genocide of African peoples. I wanted people to know that I have an identity, that I know where I come from, that any work I undertake is part of a wider process - without necessarily identifying what that process is. I had to try and strike a balance between the information I was receiving in my work and the information I needed to give out, which at times became quite draining.

ACT 3

"I trust beyond all foolish fantasies - that myself will honour myself"

Opera the plural of the latin word *opus* does not seem to adequately describe the scope of the medium. There are people who try to isolate it as an elitist experience. They are selling themselves and everyone else short. When I looked at opera as an extension of theatre, whether you call it lyric theatre or music theatre it is still part of Live Media. It has borne the Rock opera and most recently Vox opera - where the roles are created through the vocal rhythms of the singer, much in the same way an actor may create a role through the devising process. A free vocal form with a different style of notation. It is this form that I am exploring. Opera has dramatic confrontation, dialogue and music from an orchestra, it is drama that transcends mere narrative.

The medium would be richer if there was a greater cross-fertilisation between the live media and this is starting to happen. Opera is the theatre medium of the 21st century. It is interesting to observe a few trends. In the 80s, partly through GLC funding of the Arts, there was a great resurgence in black theatre. Drama schools started to accept more black actors, directors and technicians followed. I believe that this will begin to happen with opera. There are several operatic roles that require black singers. Marian Anderson, the famous contralto was the first black-woman to perform at the Metropolitan Opera House in New York in 1955. Her role - *Ulrica* in Verdi's *Un Ballo In Maschera* (A Masked Ball). *L'Africaine, Dido and Aeneas,* are examples of operas which require black singers in major roles. If we contrast this with theatre, Joseph Marcell and Rudolph Walker were the first black actors to play the role of Othello in Britain since Paul Robeson's legendary performances. We can apply the argument for integrated casting quite adequately to opera, while a director can still say that they do not 'perceive' a black actor in the role, the subtext being blatantly obvious. Music differs from the play. If the voice can take the vocal range of the role, the singer should be cast. The only colour involved should be that of the voice - is it deep, rich, light, airy. Does the role require the lower or upper register of the vocal range.

So the main problems concern the admission of black singers into the music colleges to undertake the long and arduous training required. The singers I know are encouraged to pursue careers in musicals and are openly discouraged from opera. I believe the 90s will do for opera what the 80s did for theatre. ENO has moved some way toward this by creating an Auditions Department, where they can see singers at a very early stage, offer advice and in some cases monitor their progress. But access to this information is very important and they have yet to move outside and publicise this very important initiative. There are a few well known black singers resident in Britain, Willard White, Sarah Brown; more recently Hyacinth Nicholls, Tinuke Olafimihan, Ruby Philigine and Ronald Sam. There are no directors, besides myself, that I know of.

To conclude - it has been a personal driving force that I should attain as wide an experience within live media as possible. I believe opera is an extension of theatre. What generally happens is that you can only get so far in theatre before the lure of TV and film and another series of paradoxes and barriers have to be overcome, while trying to reach the golden carrot of financial remuneration. Live media are exciting and should not be a poor relation to the mechanical media. If you believe in theatre, the power of the audience, the performers, the chemistry involved and your role as the catalyst directing a sequence/chain of reactions, then there is a real vocation. With this in mind I feel that my dreams and fantasies of where I stand in creating theatre have been enriched by working with ENO.

In the words of the great 12th century African poet Antar,

"...And the world can cast no reproach on me for my complexion: My blackness has not diminished my glory."

Nailah

One To Succeed

Nailah (often pronounced Nialah) is a Blackwomen's writing and performance group. The name derives from an Arabic word meaning 'One to Succeed' and is pronounced Ni-ee-lah. Nailah was formed in 1988 and is based at Manchester's Greenhey's Centre, in Moss Side. Nailah began as an idea to meet and share our creativity and grew into performing. It also extended into a creative writing workshop, to bring creativity to children and adults.

There are six core members with Nailah starting with: **Victoria McKenzie** then **Pauline Omoboye, Millicent Martin-Henry, Angi Weir, Elaine Fagbola**...and our youngest member **Claire-Louise Omoboye**. We all originate from a Jamaican background but with a mixture of different upbringings either from being born in Jamaica or being under the influence! Our work varies in styles, blending, overlapping or coming into stark contrast to one another. However our work is usually set in poetry form. The group started in order to give support to one another; a place to bounce ideas off, an ear to listen and share our creativity. Nailah has been an unfunded group, in terms of not receiving aid in any substantial amount. We have had very little support in the form of funds to enhance and establish Nailah. We have continued like this for the last three years. We have survived purely by our wit, our determination and our strength to keep together. You may ask why? We wanted to be recorded, remembered, as Blackwomen. To pass on our history, our language, our culture, our thoughts and our experiences - as Blackwomen growing up in Britain. Creative writing gave us that outlet, that opportunity, a way of expressing those thoughts, those feelings, that sometimes go unheard. For Nailah it was a start, an outlet, to share Blackwomen's creativity, a chance to develop their ideas through the written word.

We met as five women with an idea, we didn't think of it as anything special or important what we were doing. We wanted to write...and share our work and it grew. As we wrote, we discussed our experiences through very many aspects and angles of our lives as Blackwomen. Writing about the treatment of Blackwomen from the world, our culture, our children, ourselves and our men. We don't claim to have the answers only the views that may find an answer within the thoughts, who knows? All we knew was that we had something to say and we said it, because words are powerful. Nailah wanted to spread the word, to inform people, particularly Blackwomen who might like to join our group. We did this by producing our own magazine - NAILAH, a series of four came out and discontinued due to limited budget and no funds. It was a success in terms of producing and printing our own work and an achievement getting Nailah a voice that announced our arrival.

Our achievement as a group and as individuals (as we take the group with us as a connection), is performing with other established Black writers we admire. To perform to an audience, because without the people we wouldn't be here. Establishing Nailah in setting it up, creating an outlet to express and communicate our work. Also being able to share our work by performing within Manchester and further afield and being invited over to Ireland in June '89 to do a tour. Most recently we shared our work with a group of women from Berlin.

Nailah's ambitions are to create new avenues through creative writing, so that it can be extended in many forms. To stimulate, to share our experiences as Blackwomen, with the aid of cultural and creative arts. Our next step is to be recorded on tape, creating new work with the aid of music. To establish a permanent base that includes catering for the next generation. Where we can connect with others, produce our own and other Black writers work. To provide equipment to develop and enhance our skills, through a wide range of techniques, which will enable us to be more professional. Our ambition is to be part of history as a record, as Blackwomen, by regenerating creativity, by striking a chord...to manage that, by continuing for another year with funds, would echo our motto:

ONE TO SUCCEED.

NO REGRETS

ITS BEEN MORE THAN TWO YEARS
THAT I'VE MANAGED ALONE
I'VE COOKED AND I'VE CLEANED
I'VE ESTABLISHED A HOME
I'VE WOKE IN THE NIGHT
TO THE TEARS AND THE PAIN
I'VE TOLD THEM I'M SORRY
WHEN THEY'VE MENTIONED YOUR NAME
I'VE WIPED UP THE BLOOD
I'VE ACTED MY PART
I'VE SEWN UP THEIR CLOTHES
I'VE MENDED THEIR HEARTS
MY LIFE I HAVE ALTERED
TO REVOLVE AROUND THEIRS
I'VE PRAYED TO THE LORD
THAT HELL ANSWER OUR PRAYERS
AND WHENEVER I'M LONELY
THE CHILDREN RARELY KNOW
BECAUSE I'VE LEARNT THAT WITH PRACTICE
MY LOVE I MUST SHOW
AND WHENEVER I'M ANGRY
I'LL NEVER FORGET THAT MY MOTHER STOOD BY ME
SO I HAVE NO REGRETS

Pauline Omoboye

CREOLE IN POETRY

The Out Cast
wen mi was back a yard
in the early fifties
mi here pon di radio
how di mother country
needed we di Blacks
to come and work
after di war.

We came by di thousands -
work we could get
no where to live
houses to let
No room for the black
Di Irish or di dogs
Those were tough days.

My first experience
Chilblain toes
Frosty hands
And frost bitten nose.
Looking back so many
years had past.
We are still di
Out Cast

Victoria McKenzie

THE CARNIVAL

Did you go to the Carnival?

I did, I was playing steelband on the float. We were playing steelband with Miss Lee, one of Claremont Road School's Head Teachers.

We played a lot of songs like, Mango-walk, Liza, Don't Stop the Carnival, and lots more. You should of heard the noise; everybody clapping and shouting, it was a lots of fun, we played it, on and around streets, and in and out of Alexander Park - twenty times. Lots of bottles were on the floor. I was looking forward to that day and I'll never forget it. I didn't imagine it was going to be so busy and so noisy. Lots of people were rushing about, I saw my mum, my aunty, my brothers and sister. Though there were times when I could hardly see them because of all the people.

Then my eyes went funny; I began to see four men with whips in their hands coming towards our float, then Miss Lee said we could go and see a queen and I said what sort of queen?

Claire-Louise Omoboye

YOU

I see pictures of you young...
and I love that man,
who reaches out to me from
the crumpled photograph.

I am immediately aware
of his sensitivity,
sharpened by his pose
and caught with
the click of a lens,
he strikes me as
a humane person,
one whose soul is
forever...hidden
but allowing passion,
to run free and
claim its victim.

I'm glad I met this man,
I delight in his secrets,
his untold beauty and
warmth, inside the soul
obvious, only
to the one he loves.

Angi Weir

VEEDA

SHE GRAB HIM BY HIS THROAT
AND TELL HIM LISTEN
SHE DIDN'T JUST COME OVER HERE
TO STAND SICK PEOPLE MESSING
SHE DIDN'T NEED PEOPLE TELLING HER
TO GET OUT
AND SHE DEFINITELY
DIDN'T NEED ANY OLD MAN TO GIVE HER NOUT.

YET EVERY DAY SHE HEAR IT SHOUT
DIRTY, FILTHY, NIGGER, COON
GET BACK ON THE BOAT.

SHE HAUL HIM UP
DEN HIM BEGIN TO MAKE MORE NOISE
I'LL CALL THE POLICE TO PUT YOU IN IRONS
YOU TAKE ALL OUR JOBS
YOUR MEN PUT THEIR FILTHY HANDS ON OUR WOMEN
NOW YOU WANT TO WASH ME
WASH ME
FORGET IT ...
BRING ME A WHITE WOMAN
I DON'T WANT YOU
I'LL BATH MYSELF IF I HAVE TO

YET EVERY DAY SHE HEAR IT SHOUT
DIRTY, FILTHY, NIGGER, WHORE
GET BACK ON THE BOAT.

SHE ROLL UP HER TWO SLEEVES
AND LOOKED HIM STRAIGHT IN THE EYES
SO YOU DON'T WANT ME TO TOUCH
YOUR ACHING THIGHS
I IS QUALIFIED
AND I HAVE BETTER THINGS TO DO
BUT MY JOB IS TO TAKE CARE OF YOU
NO DOCTOR, NURSE, MATRON OR SISTER
GWARN STOP ME FROM BATHING YOU MISTER.

AND EVERY DAY SHE HEAR IT SHOUT
YOU DIRTY, FILTHY, NIGGER
GET OUT, GET OUT, GET OUT.

YOU SENT FOR MY KIND
TO WIPE UP THE MESS AFTER YOU
CAUSE YOU SAY WE'RE ANIMALS
WHO DON'T HAVE BRAINS
SO I IS HERE TO TELL YOU
WE ARE ALL THE SAME.

EVERYDAY SHE HEAR IT SHOUT
DIRTY, FILTHY, BITCH
GO HOME
NO NIGGERS ALLOWED. . .

THEN HE GIVE HER ONE THUMP
SO SHE GIVE HIM A SLAP
WHICH MADE ALL DI OTHER NURSE
STOP WITH SHOCK
HIM STARE AT HER AND MUMBLED
SOMETHING – QUICK
WHEN SHE FLING HIM BACK INTO DI BED
AND GRAB DI SOAP THINGS.

YET EVERYDAY SHE HEAR IT SHOUT
I LIKE YOU LOVE
IT'S JUST THE OTHER DARKIES
WHO SHOULD HAVE GOT BACK ON THE BOAT.

WHILE SHE WASHED HIM AND SCRUBBED HIM
RAW
SHE TELL HIM STRAIGHT
NO CARRY ON WHITELAW
CAUSE THIS BLACK NURSE WAS NOT
GETTING ILL
SO ALL IN ALL
KEEP STILL.

YET EVERYDAY SHE HEAR IT SHOUT
HELLO
GOOD MORNING
VEEDA'S ABOUT.

Millicent Martin-Henry

UNTITLED

I have heard your story a thousand times unfold.
A sad experience re-told.
As I see you
attempt to make a mould,
to dampen the spirit,
to reduce to tears.
As a woman sometimes helpless,
the only thing I can do is look
and the only thing I can do is -
wait,
for the fire to burn
to burn bright
and scream

'WOMAN IGNITE'
'WOMAN IGNITE!'
like a blazing trail
like a full moon at night
like Christmas tree lights
not made to be put out.

Elaine Fagbola

Veena Stephenson # Rubbing Culture's Nose in the Mud of Politics

As an Asian woman artist brought up, educated, and living in the West I am placed outside of the tradition and culture of the West if I am to believe what the history books tell me.

As a student I felt the vacuum of a dubious universalism and an improbable objectivity in what was on offer as Art and as History.

Gradually I learnt how to turn what Edward Said calls 'the nexus of knowledge and power' to my advantage, and in doing so I gained the freedom to decide what is relevant inside and outside that official history.

By knowledge I mean a continuing understanding - of the specific facts, interpretation, values, etc, which inform that History and which sanction its exclusions, and of how it defines itself and what it uses to define itself then proceeds to ignore.

In more concrete terms, two questions - why the art of 'non-European' cultures, and why the existence of Western women artists of the past have been consistently negated by 20th century Art History - remain as pertinent as ever because the debates which gave rise to those questions, and which attempted and still attempt to provide answers to them are continually marginalised. Consequently, students entering art education are perennially distanced either actively or by default from those debates, only enter into them by chance, with little or no help from the institutions, and having suffered damage along the way.

As for myself, I grappled my way towards some answers, albeit intellectually separating at times the experiences of being black and of being a woman, experiences which on every other level of living are inseparable.

I want to reiterate some aspects of those debates which were particular to my concerns and my attempts to, in Gayatri Spivak's words, 'trace the itinerary of the silencing'.

* * * * * *

121

The discussions on sexuality as the central theme in Anglo-American feminist theory were catalytic in the production of art by feminists, most of which focused its critique on patriarchy as it is manifest in the West, that is, as the primary source of oppression to women in the West. Whilst this may be true for white women, for Black women the crucial determining role of racism often assumes priority and the justifiably criticised institution of the family can become a source of identity and support. Due to the efforts of Black women, however, our critical position in an imperialist and patriarchal world is being recognised more and more in public forums.

Even so, the more recently influential French feminist theory, like the Anglo-American, is still dominated by a Eurocentric interest, even when applied to the Third World/Orient. Gayatri Spivak's critique of Julia Kristeva's essay ' On Chinese Women' reveals an instance of this. She says of Kristeva and others in her field that 'in spite of their occasional interest in touching the Other of the West, of metaphysics, of capitalism, their repeated question is obsessively self-centred; if we are not what official history and philosophy say we are, who then are we (not), how are we (not)?'

Elsewhere Homi Bhabha echoes Gayatri's words alongside a critique of Roland Barthes: 'There is in such readings a will to power and knowledge that, in failing to specify the limits of their own field of enunciation and effectivity, proceeds to individualise otherness as the discovery of their own assumptions.'

This is evident in the work of Nancy Spero which is informed by French theory. By appropriating images of women from non-Western cultures in an attempt to create 'woman as the universal symbol rather than the male', sexual difference is given primacy over cultural difference and the complex relations between imperialism and patriarchy are obscured.

These observations occur symptomatically because the most accessible branches of feminist theory available to women in the West, namely the Anglo-American and the French, stem from the traditions of the three most expansively imperialist nations in recent history. So whilst these theories may be at odds with the traditions in some ways, Black women cannot assume that as a consequence they are not still imbued with some of the principles of those traditions.

* * * * * *

122

VEENA STEPHENSON, "A Marriage of Inconvenience"

Returning to the subject of Art History, there are two books which are still resonant to me because of their capacity to thwart its authority.

Griselda Pollock and Roszika Parker's study 'Old Mistresses' discussed the exclusion of European women from Art History and argues that for women of a patriarchal culture the attempts to extract a separate history of art from that of men obscures the interdependant, determining role of men in that history. There are no 'grand narratives' to which women can ascribe themselves which are not also the 'grand narratives' of men. The task then is to examine the roles given within the narratives for the values they embody and the meanings they acquire, a task extensively carried out by feminist art historians in the West.

The authors assert that women 'have not acted outside cultural history ... but rather have been compelled to act within it from a place other than that occupied by men.'

Given that during the 19th century the prolific amount of work done by women artists was not ignored but given recognition in a way which was different from that of men, they focus on the question of how this difference was used and why it was necessary. By analysing the attention given to the work of women they uncover the workings of 19th century ideologies which endorse 20th century Art History's selective process.

They locate within various writings of critics and historians a construction of femininity concurrent with a change in the perceived 'persona' of the artists, and emerge with the dichotomy of woman/artist, an opposition in the meanings of 'woman' and of 'artist'. Art History, of course, concerns itself only with artists.

The deferment of meanings of notions about artistry and about womanhood, culture versus nature, high art versus craft - the interpretation of one relying on the meaning of the other - is the prop on which mainstream Art History relies.

The effect of their study is a theoretical dismantling of that prop and of the authority which negates women's art practice, without simplistically rejecting that pervading authority. We may be impatient for the material dismantling of that authority but having such a theoretical stance equips women against internalising its dictates.

Such a stance also paves the way towards a radical alteration in the criteria of understanding, assessing and producing art because it desta-

bilises the traditionally hierarchical basis used to establish the validity of a work as art.

It also disputes the supposed academic autonomy of Art History by bringing into focus the political strategy which constitutes the traditional criteria.

* * * * * *

Within heritage, culture, history, etc, it seems to me that whilst women of a patriarchal society have no separate 'grand narratives', people of an imperialised culture often do have knowledge of an era before imperialism. Also vestiges of that culture such as language, religion, certain social relations, which have not needed to change under domination continue to exist alongside new impositions.

Whilst at college I became intrigued by the evidence that Indian art seemed to mean ancient Indian art, referring only to that era before imperialism. It was/is presented either sparsely, as in generic art historical texts, or as a separate, specialised area of study.

For instance, Gombrich's much-prescribed 'The Story of Art' contains barely two pages on the entire subject. Even so he only mentions the art of Gandhara, and this only because of a supposed influence on it by Classical art which he says 'helped the Indians to create an image of their saviours.' Even in the reference section at the end of the book the most he offers is to say that by studying the Buddha image we can learn more about Eastern art 'than if we read a good many surveys of these fields.' So in a typically 'orientalist' tradition he reduces all the cultures which form the so-called East to a single stereotypical image.

* * * * * *

Partha Mitter's thorough study 'Much Maligned Monsters, History of European Reactions to Indian Art', like 'Old Mistresses', focuses its enquiry on critical attention given to art as opposed to on art itself. His study makes only slight, oblique references to the imperialist nature of the British presence in India, its approach being in the 'autonomous' realms of academic criticism.

According to Mitter, 'the formative phase in the reception of Indian Art' was between the middle of the 13th century and the end of the 17th century. From the latter part of this period onwards there was a growing

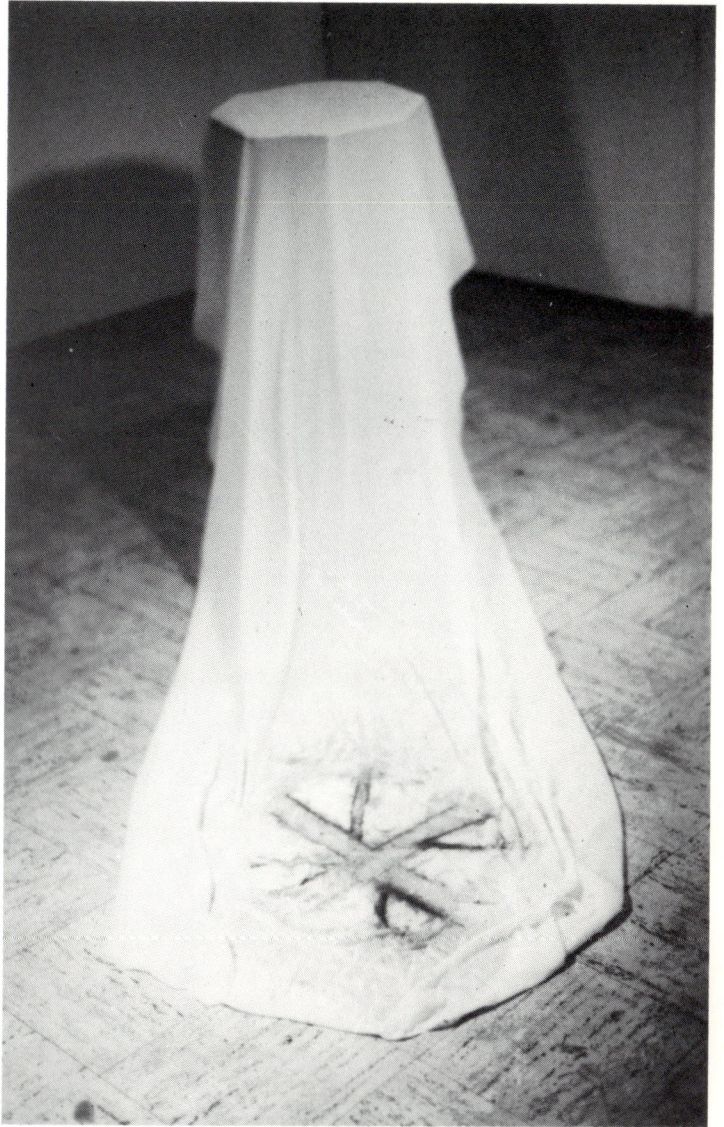

accumulation and circulation of information within various 'orientalist' discourses - religious, philosophical, ethnographical, etc - which informed Europeans such as Winckelmann and Hegel (1) in their pursuit of a universal theory on art.

Within this global, syncretic view of art Indian art was judged against the dictates of classical art which was accepted as the perfect manifestation of spirit and form. In Hegel's terms, spirit only became truly manifest in form during the classical phase and from that time set off on a progressive and developmental chain. Indian art was placed not even merely at the onset of Art History but outside of it altogether, static in development and fixed in time. This would make sense of Gombrich's exclusion of all Indian art which had no influence from the West.

To Mitter, a more valuable understanding of Indian art would be achieved by studying it 'in concrete human terms and not by presenting collective notions or metaphysical generalisations'. The early 20th century art historian, Ananda Coomaraswamy had suggested a methodology for this which he said would have to take into account contemporary forms, since they represent a continuous living tradition, and project into the past to determine their path of development. This anthropological approach, Mitter says, has not yet been taken up.

It seems obvious to me that the 'concrete human terms Mitter refers to cannot be examined without acknowledging the past and ongoing effects of imperialism, since the British involvement did much to thwart the processes of cultural production,not just intellectually as he has shown but materially as well.

A survey of the modern art books that weigh down the shelves of bookshops and college libraries reveals the logical extension of Art History's undermining of India's art of the past. That is, the complete absence of 20th century South Asian artists, not only those who practised and are still practising in their native lands, but even those who worked and received acclaim in the West.

The important point about the two books I have mentioned is that they demonstrate Art History's active and productive recognition of, rather than neglect of, the art which it disclaims. Today, Black artists and white women artists are again not ignored by critics but are increasingly subject to specific problems with the kind of recognition they receive.

Given the recent, deliberate erosion of the progress made by anti-imperialist/patriarchal movements, it remains to be seen whether or not these artists will again be written out of mainstream history as the Postmodern era progresses. However, the high level of political consciousness and activity of some of these artists, together with Postmodernism's acknowledged reliance on a recognition of difference and plurality, makes it seem possible that their contributions will be justly relevant and accessible to coming generations.

* * * * * *

NOTES

(1) From 'Much Maligned Monsters, History of European Reactions to Indian Art', Partha Mitter, Clarendon Press, Oxford 1977.

* * * * * *

BIBLIOGRAPHY

'ORIENTALISM', Edward Said, Routledge Kegan Paul, 1978

'IN OTHER WORLDS, ESSAYS IN CULTURAL POLITICS', Gayati Spivak, Methuen 1987

'THE OTHER QUESTION - THE STEREOTYPE AND COLONIAL DISCOURSE', Homi Bhabha, Screen Vol 4, 1983

'OLD MISTRESSES', Griselda Pollock and Roszika Parker, Routledge Kegan Paul 1981

'MUCH MALIGNED MONSTERS, HISTORY OF EUROPEAN REACTIONS TO INDIAN ART', Partha Mitter, Clarendon Press, Oxford 1977

Dionne Sparks

The Poetry of Theory

Blackwomen Warrior Poets Doing Our Work: Audre Lorde As Guide

In 1989 as part of my Fine Art degree I presented a thesis entitled *Black Women Creating*. My motivation was inextricably linked with my need as a Blackwoman artist to establish my identity and position within a framework of visual art practice, which in turn is webbed with my desire to know and empower my being. By clarifying for myself our collective history, politics, circumstances, products and effects of our creativity I hoped to be in a better position, knowing my revolutionary potential, to go forward with my work positively, passionately.

While stating that we have a positive history as artists I did not set out to prove our existence or to produce a list of rediscovered Blackwomen artists, innovators and leaders. But rather to explore the ways that power has survived, been inherited, and produced itself. And out of that experience to show that when that knowledge directly informs our work, our work proves to be inherently challenging and even revolutionary. In other words Blackwomen cast outside the 'norm' by virtue of our race, sex, class, sexuality have by necessity developed a depth of perception, as watchers, which makes our voices subversive and innovative, because we generally have no vested interest in the status quo. My conclusion was that this challenge and perception can carve a future for ourselves primarily, but also the world in general, which desperately needs our foresight but ironically by the same token denies it.

In the introduction to Audre Lorde's collection of essays and speeches, *Sister Outsider*, Nancy K Bereano points out that while editing the book Lorde told her that she does not write theory, "*I am a poet*", she said. "*It is precisely because she is a poet that she is on the cutting edge of consciousness*" (Bereano). As a poet she heals the unnecessary divisions between emotion and theory. Positions which white western patriarchal thought would have us believe are inherently contradictory; thus denying the emotion which informs theory presented as knowledge. In a bid towards wholeness, Audre Lorde uses the poet within, her subjective voice as Black lesbian, feminist, mother, activist, cancer survivor and more, to positively illuminate her knowing. And in the waging of that war naming herself *'warrior'* and *'Zami'* (a Carriacou, island off Grenada, name for women who work together as friends and lovers [1]). She engages me intellectually and emotionally, stopping me short of packaging anything as simple because it is convenient to do so, forcing me always to maintain a broad perspective. Her voice is at once a challenge and a comfort:

> *"Perhaps for some of you here today, I am the face of one of your fears, because I am a woman, because I am Black, because I am a lesbian, because I am myself – a Black woman warrior poet doing my work – come to ask you, are you doing yours?"* (2)

She banishes fear, knowing that in silence we are no less afraid of all that it entails to be visible. And when in the writing of my thesis (which was afterall an examination) I felt "somehow these words are too strong, I am losing perspective, over-reacting, directing a personal anger without vision", she was there with the words:

> *"... I wanted to say to the Black women of London, young Black women with whom I was in contact; it is not all in your head. Don't let them muck around with your realities. You may not be able to make very much inroad, but at least you've got to stop feeling quite so crazy."* (3)

This message enabled me to put that emotion in perspective, helped me remember that all our histories are built on slavery, that sexism and homophobia pervade our societies and that no words are too strong for that. It is a reality. Interpretations and suggestions may vary but that reality stands. Above, all, Audre helped me maintain a synthesis between poetry: emotion and theory.

I

Our societies have made their disrespect of our Blackness and our femaleness painfully clear. With that knowledge we have not only to describe our creative continuity and intellectual traditions in order to clarify and make known experience, but also to create tools for cross examining the structure of our worlds, meanings of our lives, and to find ways to disrupt, break down and rebuild towards deeper knowledge, truer understanding. Audre Lorde becomes a touchstone because of her ability to re-feel and re-think; the breadth of her being allows her to encompass so much in pristine prose and her courage sees her share it.

As Black people, as women, we must re-examine and re-embrace that which we have been taught to despise and disregard – not only literally

131

as Alice Walker did with our language in *The Colour Purple* but in ways of thinking, working and creating. This is to take up Lorde's call in *Uses of the Erotic as Power* (4). The erotic which has been selected and distorted (hence pornography) as a feminine characteristic is the "<u>yes</u> within ourselves, our deepest cravings" (5) which we have been raised to fear. By hearing and heeding this *"bloody ancient and dangerous knowing"* (Barbara Burford [6]) so we are seriously intentional, intent upon and equipped to make our lives richer.

"Poetry is the way we give name to the nameless so it can be thought" (7). To make use of words in this way, to touch the deep hidden erotic places is a serious recommendation for the uses of our work as poets, painters, weavers, builders of things; a way to turn a deeply personal activity into political progress. And, yes, land must be ploughed, our children fed and houses built, but built alongside our dreams. For the world we grow into (fight for) must be worth having as we deploy new ways of actively being.

On the precept that a problem can only be solved when it is understood, the means towards that understanding in order to bring about <u>lasting</u> change is of the utmost importance. We only settle for a *'shift in character in the same weary drama'* (8) if we hold high the grapplings of grey matter without the voice of dark feeling. So for those of us hoping to put our dreams into action Lorde concludes: *"poetry is not a luxury"* (9). For Black women our creativity, so often marginalised and sometimes absorbed by ourselves as peripheral to change, is a vital necessity and instrument of revolutionary potential. If it is true that there are no new ideas *"only new ways of making them felt "*, (10), then feel we must, and fiercely.

As warriors, as Amazons, we can only do what we can do and that should be done. For in silence we are no less afraid, anticipating contempt, judgement, censure, recognition, challenge, even annihilation but mostly being seen and heard. But in voice we grow strong; in sharing we reach difference, in fear of which we learn silence.

II

If women define their movement as one which seeks to heal, a movement towards wholeness, an abandonment of either/or thinking, then we have to address within ourselves the patterns we have learnt for dealing with difference at the hands of the destructive forces of racism, sexism and homophobia. Instead of joy at the thought of life-giving interaction we read attack and so attack first. Interacting creatively as equals across difference means vigorous reassessment and hard work. But for women to think of oppression only in terms of gender is dangerously simplistic because it ignores those women cast outside the white heterosexist 'norm' by virtue of their race, class, or sexuality. These women exist as one being, asking them to split off part of that being while dealing exclusively with gender oppression is diametrically opposed to our move, as feminists, towards wholeness. Black working class lesbian women should not have to endure this stress upon their psyche in movements committed to change. There should be some rest from the tactics of the world outside. As poet, Audre addresses coalition politics and self-preservation:

WHO SAID IT WAS SIMPLE

But I who am bound by mirror
as well as bed
see causes in colour
as well as sex

and sit here wondering
which me will survive
all these liberations (11)

In the name of sisterhood we cannot sweep over variety in a bid towards unity. That unity will soon expose itself as false. In reclaiming our herstory and creativity we cannot afford to be selective as the patriarchal telling of history has been.

The political significance of poetry itself as an art form betrays the dynamics that race, class and privilege set up between women. White women and Black women meet over anger, distrust, guilt, ignorance, and silence. We come together in love as women to form a relationship which is either life-enforcing or traumatic depending on whether we meet with courage and honesty or fear and laziness. In the words of Jackie Kay *"we are all not sisters under the same moon"* (12). We are women but we are different by virtue of our Blackness, our whiteness, our sexuality, our individuality. The world views us differently and oppresses us in accordance, making our immediate concerns vary; our ultimate concerns, however, should parallel because as feminists each woman's concern is her own. It is not by accident we find ourselves in conflict, we are not meant to come together, together we threaten an oppressive system, apart we remain suspended, ineffectual, fighting among ourselves. An interview of Audre Lorde by Adrienne Rich highlights the nature of difference and highlights a possible rich exchange between women:

> *Adrienne: ... I think it needs to be talked about, written about: the differences in alternatives of choices we are offered as Black and White women...*
>
> *Audre: ... I have a lot of conversations with you in my head ... symbolically these conversations occur in a space of Black women/White woman ... I've never forgotten the impatience that time on the telephone, when you said: "It's not enough to say to me you intuit it" ... Even at the same time that I understood what you meant, I felt a total wipeout of my modus, my way of perceiving and formulating.*
>
> *Adrienne: ... But there's a way in which, trying to translate from your experience to mine, I do need to hear chapter and verse from time to time ... If I ask for documentation, it's because I take seriously the spaces between us...*
>
> *Audre: But I'm not rejecting your need for documentation.*
>
> *Adrienne: And in fact, I feel you've been giving it to me, in your poems always, and most recently in the long prose piece ... I don't feel the absence of it now:*
>
> *There's another element in all this ... I've had a great resistance to some of your perceptions ... there's always the question: "How do I use this?" ... (13)*

Observe the poignancy of Adrienne's reaction to Audre's *"modus"*, her *"way of formulating and perceiving"*, which is her poetry. Rich, here, is in danger of losing whole well springs of creativity and information which can enrich and challenge her. As Lorde says: *"even the form our creativity takes on is often a class issue. Of all the art forms poetry is the most economical"* (14). Imagine that Audre Lorde was not able, as she has in *Sister Outsider* and *Zami: A New Spelling of My Name*, to give us *"chapter and verse"*. Imagine she had not prioritised her time to do so, did not have the time, the money, the energy, the sense of self worth to do so. Supposing she gave us only her fierce poetry. If we were unable to hear that poetry, dismissed it, as patriarchal hierarchial evaluation of art has done our patchwork quilts, for instance, if we instead said give us *"chapter and verse"*, imagine the soul we might have crushed. Luckily Audre can say: this is my language, hear it. And Adrienne can say: I know my resistance to these words, and finally realise, when in search of documentation that *"in fact, I feel you've been giving it to me, in your poems always"*. Actually, it has nothing to do with luck, it is the result of hard unflagging work in the women's movement. When women meet, in love, without fear, then, we might all conclude: *"I don't feel the absence of it now"*.

134

The same axiomatic principles which must inform Black and white women's relationships must also apply between Black women and Black men. We survived slavery, rape, lynchings, colonisation, objectification, migration. We survived, not because we remained static, not because we forgot ourselves and merged; we survived because we adapted while remembering, forging our separate identities, keeping hidden but alive our creativity, reforming and shaping our beings, being and naming above all – ourselves. As a people we have fashioned these survival tools and forged a common identity without White people. It is a deeply treasured, strong but delicate identity; it is a way to love each other. So, anything which expands upon that base, any acknowledged difference, any identity defined extra to the units is read as though it were a threat. It opens up deep vulnerabilities. The perception of threat is based upon the false premise that freedom is somehow limited and must be carved up between us; that self-definition beyond the units diminish the unit's identity. If we are to survive whole, as a people and flourish we must come together as self-actualised beings, whoever we name ourselves to be: come together; man, woman, lesbian, gay, heterosexual, colourful fibres of a strong fabric. In that multiple, strong, Black fabric we might wrap ourselves, each one, in an agenda for progress with one constant: accommodate and grow. The future requires that we do not romanticise our past, that we see where we went wrong and learn; that we fight the enemy implanted within us as well as without, so that we are not side-tracked, destroying ourselves instead of the monster which would consume us all. The future requires that we take all our best qualities and rigourously examine and disregard our worst. Of our worst qualities sexism and homophobia are pressing concerns for Black women. Audre Lorde warns:

> "It is not the destiny of Black america to repeat white america's mistakes. (Read also anywhere Black people find themselves surrounded by the values of white patriarchal society.) But we will, if we mistake the trappings of success in a sick society for the signs of a meaningful life." (15)

According to Alice Walker a womanist is "traditionally universalist" and "not separatist" (16) except "periodically for health". So while we may need to come together with women of all colours, or at other times, Black men, based on that communality, these positions are not mutually exclusive. What we live as one we must address as one. And these groups should broaden their base to encompass all our lives. We must learn when it is time to withdraw from these groups and recharge. How to distribute our energy positively so that we are not caught up as nursemaid – to others shortcomings – or educator always addressing someone else's problems and never our own.

VI

The place we are most likely to find ourselves is in ourselves. Awakening to this thought, after all the coalitions, we finally find ourselves before a hunger and a fear, deep, deep as oceans. When on the shores of this precipice do we, despite our recommendations to others, focus on the external restrictions in our lives? Pit our energy against racism, against sexism? As a rationalisation for stopping short of meeting ourselves in another Black woman.

In the exploration of this possible meeting I draw upon Audre Lorde's essay: *"Eye to Eye: Black Women, Hatred and Anger"* (17). The honesty of her piece is its driving force.

We who need each other most find ourselves, deny ourselves. The anger, a result of the hatred directed at us, is often directed most tellingly at another Black woman. Though she is not the cause of it, she is the object. We judge her critically, we are angry when she does not measure up, we are suspicious of her, jealous, wary, scared. And so desirous. Audre Lorde confesses:

> *"And if behind the object of my attack should lie the face of my own self, unaccepted, then what could possibly quench a fire fuelled by such reciprocating passions?"* (p.146)

We long for a network of support but it is not automatic because we are Black women. *"We are strong and enduring. We are also deeply scarred."* (p.151) Those of us who survive, in surviving, want more of ourselves. Yet there lies a paradox in the longing for the other that still is an effort to love; surviving and longing, with the memory of the Amazons of Dahomey in our blood, wanting more self but still obliterating that self in the face of another because we have been mated with hatred.

The pressures to conform force us to become rivals instead of sisters, to distinguish ourselves as *"the real Black woman"* (Lorde p.170). I am reminded of an incident in Toni Morrison's novel *Tar Baby*. Morrison illuminates the horizontal hostility between Black women in the confrontation between Jade and a magical *"African woman whose eyes had burnt away their lashes".* (p.44). When she spits with contempt at Jade, Jade is left feeling *"lonely and inauthentic"* (p.45) and wondering why *"the woman's insulting gesture had derailed her ... why she had wanted that woman to like her and respect her : Actually it didn't matter. When you have fallen in love, rage is superfluous, insult impossible. You mumble 'bitch', but the hunger never moves, never closes".* The desire and the distance encapsulated.

When we feel the need for each other, the loss of each other becomes unacceptable and we *"go in search of our mothers' gardens"* (Alice Walker). We go in search of ourselves. We go battling through the impositions which have been forced upon us, impositions such as the hierarchy of skin colour (linked with class privilege) and the hostility towards lesbianism. These are differences which need not keep us apart but between which we can develop a creative dialogue.

Audre Lorde wrote in 1978:

> *"Today the red herring of lesbian-baiting is being used in the Black community to obscure the true face of racism/sexism. Black women sharing close ties with each other, politically or emotionally are not the enemies of Black men".* (18)

One of the challenges that lesbianism poses to men is as a self-defined woman who does not fear male rejection. Yet that threat of rejection by men of lesbian women or women who do not distinguish themselves as anti-lesbian and therefore 'risk' being labelled lesbian, has left a silence around that experience. Ann Allen Shockley wrote in *The Black Lesbian in American Literature: An Overview*, 1979:

> *"Until recently there had been almost nothing written by or about the Black lesbian in American literature – a void signifying that the Black lesbian was a nonentity in imagination as well as reality ... It is my belief that those Black female writers who could have written well and perceptively enough to warrant publication chose instead to write about Black women in a heterosexual milieu. The preference was motivated by the fear of being labelled a lesbian, even if in some cases they were not".* (19)

So, as usual, we find ourselves set one against the other. And as usual we better deny each other before 'they' mix us up. And yet whose life are we at the risk of losing? Gloria Hull in her essay *Under the Days: The Buried Life and Poetry of Angelina Weld Grimke*, a woman who found herself unable to express her love of women, crushed and smothered, asking *"who will find me/under the days?"*, poses the question around Grimke's life. *"What did it mean to be a Black <u>lesbian</u>/poet in America at the beginning of the twentieth century"* And she offers the reply: *"First, it meant that you wrote (or half-wrote) – in isolation – a lot of which you did not show and knew you could not publish. It meant that when you did write to be printed, you did so in shackles – chained between the real experience you wanted to say and the conventions that would give you voice."* (20)

The silence to some degree is being lifted, by the efforts of women themselves, and Black lesbians are voicing their experience. Audre Lorde's *Zami: A New Spelling of My Name*, Sheba Feminist Publishers, 1984, is testimony to this: *"writing and unfolding of my life and loves"* (p.190). Through her writing we find that the life of a Black lesbian in the 1950s had not moved on that far from Grimke's:

> *"I remember how being young and Black and gay and lonely felt. A lot of it was fine, feeling I had the truth and the light and the key, but a lot of it was purely hell."* (*Zami*, p.176)

Audre found herself having to minimise her Blackness with white lesbian friends because *"we were too afraid those differences might in fact be irreconcilable, for we had never been taught any tools for dealing with them."* (p.205). And with her Black sisters in Greenwich Village it still was no source for uniting: *"too often we found ourselves sleeping with the same white women. We recognised ourselves as exotic sister-outsiders who might gain little from banding together. Perhaps our strength lay in our fewness, our rarity."* (p.177) And as for Uptown, in the land of Black people, the pressing concerns of racism and the communities lack of interest in exploring the politics of their sexuality meant most Black lesbians were closeted. *"It is hard enough to be Black, to be Black and female, to be Black, female and gay. To be Black, female, gay and out of the closet in a white environment, even in the extent of dancing in the Bagatelle, was considered by many Black lesbians to be simply suicidal. And if you were fool enough to do it, you'd better come on so tough that nobody messes with you."* (p.244)

Once again in an effort to survive, Black women found themselves unavailable to each other, touching sometimes over barricades of toughness or retreat.

I am grateful to Audre Lorde's voice of difference telling me the things I need to know, for her book *Zami: A New Spelling of My Name*, a flaming testimony to her woman-identified loving. Between the intimate, feelingful, sensuous descriptions of her lovemaking and Celie and Shug's discovery of each other in Walker's *The Colour Purple*, where we are definitely watching rather than experiencing two women make love, it is obvious that Audre's life experience is a torch to see ourselves by and allows us as heterosexuals to feel the lesbian in ourselves, which we cannot afford to lose. It is a fierce book, and true. It brings to life the need and the right of Black women to live where we choose, and to share and love across sexualities, which we must not turn away from. Turning away from that life, conceding to her isolation, we invisibilise her and force her to live the best way she can, *"chained between the real experience"* and *"the conventions that would give (her) voice"* (Gloria T. Hull). Some are hoping she will become a nonentity in reality, and others, so removed from the concept of her life actually find her a *"nonentity in imagination as well as reality"* (Ann Shockley). But we know she lives and we know the value of her life to each, herself, ourselves; and without that life there remains a gaping hole in our sisterhood and we are diminished. Audre Lorde meets the issue head on:

> *"I feel not to be open about who I am in all respects places a certain kind of expectation on me. I'm just not into meeting anymore ... I am not a piece of myself. I cannot be simply a Black person and not be a woman too, nor can I be a woman without being a lesbian... What happens when you narrow your definition to what is convenient, or what is fashionable, or what is expected, is dishonesty by silence."* (21)

At the beginning of this section I posed the question: Do we, despite your recommendation to others, focus on the external restrictions in our lives, as a rationalisation for stopping short of meeting ourselves in another Black woman? And in that journey, the visceral search, seeking out all those things that would fragment us while holding on to the individual self, Lorde has shown me that to progress as a group we become mothers to ourselves; nurturing ourselves we nurture each other. By recovering that which is natural which has been stolen – our love of each other, ourselves – we begin to heal our isolation. We have to believe in our worth before we touch each other, which is difficult in an environment bent on denying our needs; but not impossible. Moving beyond a veneer of self-worth, learning our possibilities and differentiating between our needs and our capabilities and what the world outside would drive us towards; moving towards a celebration of our successes and a tenderness with our failings, we claim power over who we choose to be and acknowledge the relativity in our lives. But always knowing that without that empowerment we cannot change a thing.

I have come around again to the reasons for my journey into Black women's creativity. I am a Black woman searching out my power. I am

139

a Black woman searching. I am an inheritor of strong spirits and I have work to do. Those Black women artists addressing our herstory, our lives, realities, our hopes, our fears and dreams are telling it like it is, which may be hard for some to hear, but we can tell it no other way. We are not creating for effect, we are not attempting to be omnipotent, universal ogres, hiding behind the pretence of unclouded eyes. We look <u>through</u> our anger, our pain, our fierce love, whatever it is, we look through those clouds, gather the raindrops, the storms and the sun and tell it like we see it. Because the way <u>we</u> see it is valid, and we insist upon the particular as our strength. We will not look away out of fear. Perhaps then heads may turn and see us turning, turning tides, crashing, breaking down the stone. Then we may begin. We may begin. One principle our foundation:

"The master's tools will never dismantle the master's house" (22)

NOTES

1. Audre Lorde, *Zami: A New Spelling of My Name*, Sheba Feminist Publishers, 1982, p.255.

2. Audre Lorde, *Transformation of Silence into Language and Action*, paper delivered at the Modern Languages Association's 'Lesbian and Literature Panel', Chicago, Illinois, Dec 1977, reprinted *Sister Outsider*, The Crossing Press, 1984, p.40-44.

3. Audre Lorde, interviewed by Pratibha Parmar and Jackie Kay *Charting the Journey, Writings by Black and Third World Women*, ed. Shabnam Grewal et al, Sheba Feminist Publishers, 1988.

4. *Uses of the Erotic: The Erotic as Power*, 1978. *Sister Outsider*, as above.

5. Ibid.

6. Barbara Burford, from the poem in *A Dangerous Knowing: Four Black Women Poets*, Sheba Feminist Publishers, undated.

7. Audre Lorde, *Poetry is Not A Luxury*, first published in *Chrysalis: A Magazine of Female Culture*, No. 3, 1977, *Sister Outsider*, as above.

8. See note 4 p.59.

9. See note 7.

10. Ibid.

11. Audre Lorde, *Who Said it was Simple, In the Name of the Father. The Poetry of Audre Lorde*, Jerome Brooks, *Black Women Writers*, ed. Mari Evans, Pluto Press, 1985. p.272.

12. Jackie Kay, *We Are Not All Sisters Under The Same Moon* , see note 6.

13. An Interview: 'Audre Lorde and Adrienne Rich', see note 2, p.103.

14. Audre Lorde, *Age, Race, Class, Sex: Women Redefining Difference*, paper delivered at the Copeland Colloquium, 1980, see note 2, p.116.

15. Audre Lorde, *Sexism: An American Disease in Blackface*, first published as *The Great American Disease*, in *The Black Scholar*, vol. 10, no. 9 (1979), in response to *The Myth of Black Macho: A Response to Angry Black Feminist* by Robert Staples in *The Black Scholar*, Vol. 10, no. 8.

16. Alice Walker, *In Search of Our Mothers' Gardens*, The Women's Press, 1984. For a definition of womanist p.xi.

17. Audre Lorde, see note 2, pp.145-175.

18. Audre Lorde, *Scratching the Surface: Some Notes on Barriers to Women and Loving*, first published in *The Black Scholar* , Vol 9, no. 7 (1978). Reprinted in *Sister Outsider*, see note 2.

19. Ann Allen Shockley, *The Black Lesbian in American Literature: An Overview*, from *Conditions: Five. The Black Women's Issue*, New York, ed Lorraine Bethel and Barbara Smith, April 1980. Quoted by Alice Walker in *Breaking Chains and Encouraging Life*, 1980. 'In Search ...' see note 16.

20. Gloria Hull, *Under the Days: The Buried Life and Poetry of Angelina Weld Grimke*, printed in *Conditions: Five* and reviewed by Alice Walker as above, note 19.

21. Audre Lorde, *My Words Will Be There, Black Women Writers*, ed Mari Evans, Pluto Press, 1985, p.262.

22. Audre Lorde, *The Masters Tools Will Never Dismantle the Masters House*, comments at 'The Personal and The Political Panel', Second Sex Conference New York, 1979 printed in *Sister Outsider*, see note 2, p.110.

SONIA BOYCE , "Mr. Close-friend of the Family", 1st exhibited *Thin Black Line*, ICA 1985, reproduced in *Thin Black Line* catalogue, UFP 1989, available from UFP, price £5 p & p free.

Pat Agana

Training For Life

A transcript of a speech

Let me begin by saying that I have come here in full awareness of the wealth of personal experiences present in this room, the numerous professionals and the skills that we collectively possess. I aim only to focus your minds for a few moments on the issue at hand and encourage all present to acknowledge that we have here and now what is needed to make change.

I am hear today to talk about Child Abuse which can be broken down into four categories.

CHILD SEXUAL ASSAULT:

The use of children for the sexual gratification of an adult or an elder person, where the person or child's knowledge is such that they are unable to give informed consent.

PHYSICAL ABUSE:

Where a child is subjected to acts by an adult that cause the child physical damage.

NEGLECT:

Where an adult fails to care adequately for the emotional, spiritual, physical and educational needs of the child. This may be deliberate or because of the adult's own disabilities or lack of information.

EMOTIONAL ABUSE:

Where a child is continually subjected to situations or verbal encounters which lower the child's self esteem, cause the child distress which ultimately affects the quality of his/her life and future interactions.

Child abuse may be one or any combination of these. Each one of these areas is cause for grave concern, but today I choose as my focus; Child Sexual Assault, for it is the least discussed within our community and I feel strongly that if we do not address it ourselves it will be addressed by

143

various institutions on our behalf. Already I have been asked to participate in a television production about Black people and child sexual assault, invited to submit information as to why so few Black men are in prison on charges relating to sexual offences against children. The researcher apparently completely oblivious to the fact that a disproportionate amount of Black men have and are being incarcerated for numerous other offences already, without this new drive to add to the list. As we have seen in the past there are numerous people out there waiting to equate our struggle with theirs and straining at the leash in an effort to speak on our behalf.

In October 1989 I attended the Caribbean Regional Conference on Child Abuse and Neglect. That was an eye opener. Quite apart from the experience of being in the presence of some three hundred African professionals from all over the Caribbean with only seven Europeans in evidence. Here a serious and concerted effort was being made to address the issue of Child Abuse. This was held by the conference to fall into two major categories, child abuse perpetrated by governments' failure to admonish its communities and that perpetrated by individuals within and outside families. In that conference some thirty Africans who had been sexually abused as children came together to discuss their experience. All the evidence I needed that it is an issue which concerns us here in Britain.

Child sexual abuse is not a new phenomenon. Each and everyone of us can relay stories from our childhood about particular individuals in our communities who were said to be strange or it was said that they were the father of their daughter's child. These tales may have been whispered but we all know of them.

The effects of child sexual abuse include behavioural problems, educational deficiency, eating disorders, mothers giving birth to sons and making their lives hell because they are frightened they may grow up to be abusers. Families keeping girl children under strict regimes only to realise years later that the trusted friend of the family had been abusing the daughter for years. Unexplained suicides, teenage pregnancies, prostitution, children confused about their sexuality.

Men sexually abuse girls and boys. The majority of the men found responsible have been heterosexual. Women have been known to sexually abuse children though the majority of reported cases have been perpetrated by men. Women are more likely to emotionally abuse children. It is only now that information is beginning to come to the fore

144

on the sexual abuse of men. Men are however less likely to report sexual assault upon them as youths for reasons of social conditioning. Those men that do come forward present a ray of hope for young boys who are currently being sexually abused for they will be encouraged to speak out and be able to gain support from adult men who have survived.

WHY DOES IT HAPPEN? THERE ARE MANY THEORIES:

One is that the abused child's powerlessness is a direct consequence of abuse. A girl child in western society is socialised into powerlessness, which may be reintroduced by sexual abuse. The idea exists that every girl goes through such an experience in their life and so it is acceptable. The girl in growing to be a woman is taught thus to know her place. For the boy that has been sexually abused however, the dynamic is different. In order to be M.A.N. in this society he has to somehow reverse the process (boys cannot be raped), he has to find some way to exert his power over someone or choose a mode of social interaction which does not adhere to existing values.

It is sometimes attributed to mental disturbances of the perpetrator. A 'temporary lapse' which however does not explain why statistics indicate that on average the child molester in his lifetime will offend 32.5 times against boys and 42 times against girls (American).

The judiciary attributes the cause to women: the mother who works nights; is suffering from longterm illness or has a nervous breakdown. The underlying theory here being that men have a rampant sexuality which must be satisfied at all costs. An insult to male intelligence I think!

Religion attributes it to idleness. Sociologists attribute it to race and class. Feminists attribute it to men. Politicians attribute it to the breakdown of the family. Yet facts indicate that it is the family that maintains secrets, the cause/causers are only relevant to the degree that they can offer a solution.

The most disturbing feature of child sexual abuse is the degree to which it is sanctioned in institutions and social behaviour in this country.

The ethos of instant gratification which permeates today's western civilization. A legal system that gives minimal sentences for rape and child sexual assault while giving major sentences to crime against property. Newspapers magazines and book publications that promote the use of women and children as sexual objects all contribute to the silence and secrecy surrounding sexual assault of children. A social system that condemns a woman who leaves a relationship. A legal system that believes the confessions of childmolesters and rapists but will not act to protect the child. VD (venereal disease) clinics which see hundreds of children from 2 to 16 and because of laws surrounding confidentiality take no action that will protect the child.

So where do we as Africans fit into all of this. The statistics are not about us. We are here today to build structures which are Afro-centric – that will safeguard and build new values.

The fact is that rape and sexual assault of children exists in our communities amongst our African peoples. We will not take time today to debate when or why this became a reality. It is here in our midst. Many of us in this room today know individuals, directly or indirectly, who under a guise of righteousness have abused the respect of women, men and children. People often do not expose these people for fear, sheer embarrassment or pain. But our silence gives them too much power and undermines the things that we are working for. They also stand as misrepresentations of what African manhood is about.

I often hear arguments that men are no longer able to touch their daughters for fear of being accused of sexual assault, we are no longer allowed to chastise children for fear of being accused of abuse. HOW REAL IS THIS? In my experiences it is highly unlikely that a warm caring relationship between a parent and child which respects a child is likely to be any different because of the publicity around sexual assault. It is an issue of conscience whether or not we feel at ease with our children and an issue of our practical responsibility.

The way forward then is integral to the purpose of this conference today. We have a need to ensure the physical, spiritual, emotional and educational well-being of ourselves and our children and hence all Africans abroad. To make change we must start with ourselves.

Addressing child sexual assault as with child abuse means for us first to address racism.

When Africans were first enslaved it was necessary for Europeans to evolve a philosophy of justification. In the process well over 75 million Africans were left at the bottom of the sea. These basic assumptions inform this society's interaction with us to this very day. Ideas which have become enshrined in this country's culture.

we are not quite human;
we are highly sexual beings; we know nothing about parenting:
we have no language, no culture, no traditions;
being Black we are synonymous with evil;
we are aggressive;
we know * * * *
we are assumed to be physical not intellectual
This being stated they were able to argue that enslavement was a civilising process. Today all interactions with white institutions are governed whether overtly or covertly by these principles. We in turn in service to these principles either live to them (this is my place and I shall be good at it) or we militate against their principles. The result being that we are identified as different from the rest; and successful, mad or bad.

For us to survive whole, we need to rethink our value systems and forge an Afrocentric perspective.

The abused child feels responsible for what has taken place. The abused child feels dirty, the abused child feels alone, the abused child feels angry, the abused child feels negative about themself and all these feelings feed into the impact. An African child who has been sexually abused can confuse this whole experience with what it is to be an African, the outcome is very often a compounded self hate.

Our task is not to run from the existence of child sexual abuse, but to accept that it is a reality and thus listen and investigate information that children bring to us.

I am advocating a conscious taking of responsibility for the welfare of our children by both men and women whether we are the ones who gave birth to them or not. Those adults who commit these crimes against the community need help or are consciously involved on a mission of self destruction. Either way they have to be exposed and made to take responsibility for their actions.

In the last twenty years, I have known of men, men who are known to many of us here, men who have and continue to rape and physically abuse women, men who have and continue to molest children. Women and children who are alone in their suffering. Yet they have been sheltered in our midst because we have not the systems in place to address the moral and spiritual health of our community. Very often the individuals responsible are the most well read and spout the most

147

rhetoric. Political consciousness then is obviously not enough to safe-guard a whole human being.

Each and everyone of us is capable of making a mistake, but as Walter Rodney said *"Once may be considered an incident, twice a coincidence but thrice is a definite tendency."*

My brothers and sisters, I am sorry there are more questions than answers. I am, however, confident that among us here today there are more than enough suggestions to begin to address the issues raised. I hope that I have given you all sufficient food for thought and that you will generate workshops, discussions and writings around these issues.

In the meantime, may I proffer some solutions: Children have a right to be protected and that protection should appropriately come from adults. Parenting is a lifetime commitment and a responsibility which cannot, by any stretch of the imagination, be taken on by one person. It is both an individual and collective responsibility.

How can we ensure our children's safety? We need to LISTEN to our children and show them that we VALUE the contribution they have to make. We need to respect the fact that they are our future. We need to appreciate them for what and who they are as well as who and what they may become. We must love them unconditionally in their success and in their failures. We must teach them how to make decisions. We must work to make their childhoods happy. We must guide them and set realistic boundaries. We must always expect the best of them. We should be prepared to learn from them. We must understand that play, and our part in it as responsible adults, is an integral part of any child develop-ment.

We should allow them to express their feelings in a safe, caring environ-ment so that they do not have to turn away from their cultural traditions to find expression.

Lastly, and most importantly, a clear thinking adult who is open to reason; who is prepared to ask for help; who is prepared to admit their own failings and respond to changes is the most beneficial support and teacher any African child may have.

In conclusion I want to say in all humility that your presence here shows me that there is a way forward.

The Asian Women Writers' Collective

At The End Of A Greenhouse Summer

Every Wednesday in a small reading room in the Women's Centre at Holborn we meet – a core group of some 8-10 Asian women. Today there is a new person in our midst but our animated talk hushes as one member picks up a carefully word-processed sheet of A4. "You know I'm hopeless at reading…" But as she starts, the words begin to fill up all our uncertainties…

COLD, WET MINORITY

now
recently
a kind pale soul said to me
'don't be silly
Black people aren't a minority in the world'
true
I thought
but then again each day
I step onto my cold england doorstep
my eyes don't stretch wide enough to
take in
all those
warm masses
curving darkly
round the globe.

still
I got mildly cheerful
when racist ideologies got a little confused
at the end of a greenhouse summer
shouting at dark-haired white people in the street
'Oi, you, why don't you go back where you belong!'

This sharing of our writing and the ensuing critical feedback is one facet of the Asian Women Writers Collective, a London-based group of women who meet weekly to discuss creative work. Parallel to this are other activities of the Collective such as skill-sharing workshops for members, on anything from comedy writing to projecting your voice for public readings, and the constant schedule of readings and workshops in the local community. In recent months we have also made new links with communities outside London – in Manchester, Tameside and Brighton.

The Asian Women Writers Collective was started in 1984 as the Asian Women Writers Workshop, mainly due to the efforts of one member, Ravi Randhawa, who had managed to get the support of Black Ink publishers and some funding from the GLC (Greater London Council). Since its inception, the membership has grown and we now have some 20-30 members. The Collective receives financial support from Greater London Arts and Lambeth Council.

In 1988, the *Women's Press* published *'Right of Way'*, an anthology of short stories and poems by the Collective. When we set out to get an anthology of our work published, most of us had never been published before. Even fewer of us had set aside time to devote exclusively to writing, so we were only able to write in what we believed to be inspired bursts of energy. Therefore, an anthology seemed to be well suited to us and it also seemed the best way to represent all the talent in the workshop.

The Collective was the first of its kind for Asian women writers in Britain, and was meant to draw out any isolated women who wanted to write but needed a supportive environment to achieve this. The need for this kind of group was poignantly expressed in one of our early meetings when a younger woman, confronted an older woman who had just finished reading a moving story with the question, "Where were you when I was growing up?" Did it take that long for 'immigrants' to feel settled and strong enough to want to express, re-order and interpret their reality for themselves and society at large? We were also working in a vacuum; there seemed to be no precedents to which we could refer. A few Asian women had been published, but not enough to set up parameters which we could break or work within. Organising as a group gave us visibility, credibility and access to institutions, publishers and other groups in the community. The workshop gave us the confidence to approach publishers, which as individuals we might never have done. It answered the vital question that haunted all of us: is my writing of any interest or use to anyone else?

In its short history, many women came and went but now a core group of around ten women appears to have crystallised. We also have a few members from outside London who regularly send in their work. We have tried not to make the stability of our core group seem intimidating for new members and constantly invite new people to join us.

Most of us have found the workshop process useful. It is a stimulus to write when all other methods of self-discipline have failed. You know that, within a few weeks, the other members will be looking askance at

150

you if you have not brought any writings to the workshop. It must be said that many of us are in full-time employment and almost all of us have families to contend with, which means that time devoted to writing has to be negotiated. As this is not a paying proposition, our bargaining power is considerably weakened.

Suggestions and criticism provide new perspectives, new directions for work which might have dried up in your mind. What critical standards we are, and should be, using are questions that have led to heated but unresolved debates. We tend to use personal statements to reduce the edge of criticism, so that a writer's work is not subjected to some implicit, universal, objective criteria; such as poetry having to have complex imagery. We have to ask who formulated these criteria, and are they relevant to us, as Asian women writing in a country where writers are recognised as great on the terms of white middle-class male critics. How do we evolve our own standards without falling into the trap of venerating every word written by Black women purely because their disadvantaged position has reduced them to a marginality?

Though we see ourselves as British-based Asian women, not all of us were bred and born here, and we brought with us different cultural and literary influences. This affected our critical responses. Some of us found it difficult to appreciate translations of Urdu or Bengali poetry. Anglicised responses to the style being flowery or sentimental demanded discussion and contexualisation. Short stories which were rooted in the literary traditions of the sub-continent were considered to have abrupt endings; further discussion revealed that the marked ambiguity of the endings was common to our literary traditions. Criticism of work seemed to be much easier on political grounds. Positions were clearly drawn and we were able to speak about the content; for example, this is classist, patronising, communalist, heterosexist, or whatever. But how did we respond to work where there were no political disagreements but where, for instance, a poem simply failed to move you? As a group, we are constantly struggling to define our literary criteria so that it does not merely reflect our own conditioned responses to 'good' and 'bad' styles of writing. This does not mean that there was always a consensus of political views. When we made the transition from a workshop to a collective, political arguments arose from the name we should give ourselves. Some of us suggested that we should call ourselves 'black' women to show our alignment with that part of the movement which believes that Asian and Afro-Caribbean women face a common oppression and that the way ahead is to fight together. Others felt that they had been squeezed out of Blackwomen's writing groups where the women

151

were predominantly Afro-Caribbean and the implicit attitude was that the term 'black' belonged to them. Yet others felt that there were cultural differences which would make it difficult to respond critically and knowledgeably to Afro-Caribbean writing and vice versa. There was also the feeling that there was no Asian women's forum and that in order to encourage young women writing for the first time to join, our composition should be reflected in our name. Consensus was reached when it was said that we should work closely with Blackwomen's groups and participate in all events for Blackwomen writers.

The second big debate was sparked of by the word 'women' in the name. Were we not feminists, should it not be Asian feminist writers? Many women felt that the word feminist had been sullied by the exclusiveness and racism of white middle-class women, therefore, was no longer a useful term for us. There were such differences in our understanding of feminism that in any case the term would have been completely meaningless as a way of selecting new women to become members of the workshop. Also, it would have meant overturning the original idea of the workshop, which pre-dated many of us: the forum should be available to all Asian women. That these issues were not resolved was frustrating but also led to interesting debates in which work was viewed in a political context and the relationship between writing and politics became clearer. The very fact that we needed to set up a group for a particular section of society was an enunciation of the political realities that normally excluded women like us. Consciousness developed through the workshop process of our need to write in a particular way, to take into account our own class position when writing, and to recognise the way in which this distorted our perceptions, and of our need for positive but realistic images of Asian women. A resolution was passed that we, as a group, were opposed to racist, communalist, classist and anti-lesbian attitudes and writings, so that there was some agreement, some given assumptions, upon which we could build further.

Unfortunately, working towards our first anthology and now our second, has taken up a lot of our energy though this has also provided us with an impetus to write. We have received so much new writing that we now have a 'readings' collection of work that has been approved for public readings. We also invite women writers to talk about their work and to run workshops for the collection, for example Sita Ramamurthy conducted a workshop on 'Performance Reading' and Afshan Malik on 'Comedy Writing'. Amongst ourselves we rotated the running of workshops where we set each other exercises. We found this very useful. It shattered all our romantic notions about writing only when inspired. It showed us that if we worked at something, even when we were exhausted after our day's work, we could come up with a fairly readable piece. It also redefined writing so that we saw it as a craft, a tool which could be honed and perfected with effort; it chased away any elitist notions of being born with a talent. In a world where literary skills are limited, we were forced to recognise the privilege of our positions.

Most of our writing had been shared mainly by public readings, and this affected our style of writing. We felt that we had to be short, punchy, direct, rhetorical and dramatic. As our method of operation in the workshop was also reading our material aloud to each other and then discussing it, we never looked at our writing from the point of view of the written page, where it is possible to hold the attention of the reader with more complex structures. What was boring when read aloud for thirty minutes looked quite different when read privately. This became important when we launched the idea of an anthology: we had to see pieces not merely in terms of performance.

Since our first publication *Right of Way*, many more women have become involved in the Collective and, inevitably, the core group has changed accordingly. Our second anthology therefore aims to reflect many of the new perspectives and we are now liaising with publishers.

The past year has also seen a growth in our activities in the community mainly as a result of the Collective now having two part-time workers; one for administration and another for outreach. The Collective has held workshops in schools, community centres and colleges that have inspired both young and old to develop their writing. Sometimes our presence acts as a spring-board for smaller groups to be created. We have also gained more visibility by public performance readings particularly during the Feminist Book Fortnight and our annual readings event *Mehfil* continues to attract new audiences. But the precariousness of our funding situation is a problem that is looming over us as we, like many other Black groups, are having to face up to the huge cuts in arts funding by local authorities. The future we know is going to be different. But we aim for our strength, as Asian women, and as writers, never to be diminished.

NINA EDGE, "Snakes and Ladders"

Nina Edge

Your Name Is Mud

In talking about 'craft' practice and black craftswomen a dance must be stepped through a sludge of definition, misinformation, appropriation and assumption. A series of conversations with foundation arts students, arts graduates and post graduates reveals plenty of sludge amongst a privileged group who have been the recipients of a generous slice of the United Kingdom's art 'Education' cake. Having gorged for some time on the sweet taste of the 'knowledge' available from large British institutions, those trained in the 'Fine Arts' emit an acrid belch of superiority on the subject of their craft. Their homes are often sumptuously hung, not with the finest of eurocentric defined Fine Art, or even the craftiest of Crafts Council defined craft, but with Javanese batik, Indian embroideries, West African Adire, and selected ex-colonial produce. Objects of this nature in the sludge ridden book of definitions are not even craft, are less than craft, are merely *ethnic*. Simple practice without analysis may be seen to be part of the craft tradition; crafts people and their wares not being subject to literary criticism in the way that arts people are and historically have been.

To engage in activities defined as 'craft' without thinking about it might appear to be a merry dance but the sludge is always there to be slipped up in. In order to pass by without getting something sticky on your feet it is wise to be aware of the nature of these definitions, misinformations, appropriations and assumptions. It is perhaps a shame to divert attention and energy away from the act of making and being, toward analysis of how your makings and be-ing (what you make and who you are) are received by those who are empowered to see them. It takes account of what the products are called and where they rest. If they have come to rest through the act of sale to a stranger then, what was their price?, and, in what currency were they purchased? Who has enough food to exchange goods for a piece of baked earth or strands of the seed of cotton, and why are they inclined to buy handmade objects at all when manufactured goods look safer, may be guaranteed, and will almost always be cheaper?

Are there differences in the experience of handling and owning materials that have been processed by hand and those processed by machines, tools and computers? It could be said that a major function of handmade ceramic ware, individually thrown mugs and bowls, is to aid the transition into the automated computer age. A comforter in a world of

155

numbers and bar codes. From the time of the resurrection of handmade table ware in the United Kingdom to the present day, the booms in sales of craft ware follows closely the introductions of major technological changes and their ever increasingly felt effect on all aspects of life. Outside of the 'high craft' venues: galleries and museums, the most likely locations for the purchase of handmade wares are regions where there are tourist industries. What better way to prove that you have been somewhere in a consumer culture, than to buy something made locally whilst you are there. The United Kingdom's tourist industry relies to an incredible extent on a nostalgia, a re-construction of the past, particularly a rural past without tears, bloodstains or nasty smells. It is connected to a desire to paint an all white picture of Britain, a Britain before 'immigration' an insular idea of what Ye Olde British culture and produce was.

Until the late eighties emergence of a 'Green' lobby it was cosily believed that food production went on in a 'time honoured' manner and that the countryside was free from sin, modernisation or modern problems. The dream of pastoral heaven includes in it an attitude towards the type of objects it is believed have always been made there, as well as beliefs about the type of people who make them; decent simple folk. If the role of the artist in British culture has been reduced to the performing monkey of the powerful, living publicly the lives that are not quite nice, then perhaps craft has been reduced to the fulfilment of the forbidden dreams of workers from the mechanised workplace. In a country where engineering has been a major power tool the love and respect of 'skill' and 'craftsmanship' are not likely to disappear as quickly as the workplaces which bred them. The adult education programmes of the sixties enabled large numbers to access various craft media on courses which were marketed both as relaxation and therapy to counter the fast new world as well as the potential means of escaping it, of returning to eden with a recognisable skill which used creative and visual thinking to an extent unknown even in the days of pre-robotic engineering.

Of course with the exception of war efforts women were allowed scant access to the skills of engineering in the heavy sense. Their responsibilities as workers in the service sector as well as in the home provided them with a different experience in terms of fabrication. Stretching money for food necessarily engaged women in turning their skills of fabrication into cash. The most obvious example in this area is sewn and knitted textiles which used to, and continue to, provide income for people unwilling, or unable to participate in factory production and its allied service industries. Financial returns may be slim but the experience of buying, selling and costing within a practice which in Thatcherism is termed 'small business' continues to be of immense value to female makers. Such businesses are part of what could be broadly termed women's culture and are more highly developed within some class groupings than others. During the sixties craft booms there were women who were ready to start making craft from a different starting point.

In a market where it is standard practice that the labour of women is purchased for less than that of men and the labour of black women often bought for less than that of white, what value is likely to be placed on objects made and sold by women? Is the buyer made aware of the identity of the maker and is the purchase as much to do with buying a little bit of a named crafts person as it is to do with fancying one of those objects to take away? Sales people in craft venues are asked more questions about the identity of the makers of craft ware, than sales staff selling machine manufactured goods. Try asking in High Street stores if goods on display were designed by men or women, black designers or white and this becomes obvious. Notions about the un-named craftsman imported from Japan by Mr Bernard Leach in the thirties seem to be long gone within contemporary crafts practice. Or are they? It can be argued that many more people are crafts people in the United Kingdom today than might appear obvious. In particular there are many more crafts women and large numbers of them are black. Much of the hand-worked lace and crochet work, embroidery and bead work which essentially sells garments at the top end of the clothing industry, is made by women who see only piece meal rates in exchange for work which cannot be performed by machines. Throughout India, the Caribbean and the United Kingdom highly skilled textile workers are exploited at home despite the highly developed skill and knowledge implicit in their work. It would be hard to envisage The Crafts Council of Great Britain acknowledging them as crafts people worthy of registering on their register.

This is a place on a list reserved for some other sort of maker by hand. It might appear logical to assume that acknowledgement by The Crafts Council is dependant on the maker being the owner of the whole means of producing the whole article, and being the sole maker from start to finish. (The piece working craftswomen return collars, cuffs, borders etc. to the boss who arranges for their marrying to a garment and a buyer.) However the register(s) of 'real' crafts people does not bear this out as some of those registered work with often un-named assistants. Some have a minimal tactile relationship with their wares and work more as designers than makers. It might be logical to assume that they are not recognised as crafts women because their face does not fit. A certain status needs to be attained in addition to a certain level of craft. The one

157

without the other will not work. For example, an applicant to The Crafts Council will need to be literate in the language of English and have access to the tools and technology of photography. A flick through back copies of prestigious crafts magazines and catalogues of prestigious marketeers reveal a disproportionate number of men working with what are seen to be traditional craft materials, making big money, big headlines, and big names for themselves. Often their work is no more worthy of such acclaim (whatever it's worth) than that of women who have been practicing in that field, in those same materials and stunningly skilfully.

A further example of this appropriation can also be seen in the media which the art establishment are now prepared to see as the stuff which real art is made of. During the eighties a number of women students in colleges throughout the United Kingdom were using paper, cloth and soft woven materials on sculpture courses, some continuing to do so as professional artists. Having had their courage suitably ridiculed and penalised the ideas and media used have been appropriated by male artists who through the mystical power of maleness are somehow able to gain access to major venues, reviews, acclaim and remuneration for copying 'what the girls did'. So traditionally female crafts, for which they have traditionally been underpaid are prone to being worth real money if they are undertaken and re-marketed by men. This could be due to a kind of tunnel vision which men collectively have developed towards anything which women make, although the powerfully obvious influence of women's 'ware' on men's 'art' to an extent denies this.

This tunnel vision relates more succinctly to recognising the skill and artistry involved. In the homes of some men, powerful in the art world, ceramic vessels are to be found, both hand and factory made. Almost without exception the lines and colours painted onto factory wares, the life perhaps in the machine ware is painted by women. Fine and good work. What is not fine and good in the '90s, and has never been fine and good in the history of British ceramics, is the price the women are paid for their painting. Reducing the term painting to the term decorating is no excuse for paying the workers (whose mark making prowess sells the pots) piece-rates and forcing them to work in uncomfortable and dangerous environments. Even now it is possible to witness a handful of men enjoying well-daylit and comparatively well-ventilated painting rooms whilst in the same factory women sweat over piece-work in dark or artificially lit decorating chambers inhaling the brain and lung damaging fumes of fat oil. Essentially they are performing the same task. In no way do their wages reflect this. Later the women's painting influences and inspires the 'real' men painters who work with pigment on canvas and

158

enjoy the real status and financial rewards of being named *artists*. These women who paint in the factories are not defined as artists or as crafts women; they get called workers. Their names are not apparent on their wares but rather their number, for purposes of piece-work remuneration and, of course, quality control. Since these women are not called painters, artists or crafts women it seems that handwork is not necessarily craft. Meanwhile back in the real craft world photo-processed screen printed transfers applied to hand or factory produced ware may be called craft; hence craft need not necessarily involve handmaking.

The delineation between that which is described (and hence paid for as art) and that which is described as craft looks on first sight to be purely based on media used. It remains to be seen whether the definitions in current use are either accurate or useful. Clay, cloth, silver, wood, wool, all sound like craft media. Of course if a practitioner with a fine arts qualification uses media which sound crafty they are not making *craft*, but making *art in innovative media*! If a practitioner with no qualifications, or a craft/design qualification uses crafty materials they are making craft and their work is priced and marketed accordingly. The difference in pricing runs approximately like this – Art is worth whatever you can get for it, whatever you say it is worth. Craft is priced according to size, inherent value of materials used, numbers of hours used in production, in relationship to overheads. Craft work becomes more expensive if the maker is dead, ageing or already collected by an international market of craft buyers, i.e. nearing art through virtue of finding a place in international art/currency transactions. One of the problems with attempting to define craft on the basis of media is the illogical nature of defining what something is, through merely noticing what is has been made of.

> I make things out of clay and colour, cloth and colour, and words. If a person makes things out of canvas and colour they can be called *artist*. If a person makes things which are not vessels out of clay they might be called *sculptor*. The same person making clay vessels is more likely to be trapped in the definition of *craftsman*, or sometimes in these modern times *craftsperson*.

> Sticks and stones can break your bones but names can cost you up to £250 in hanging fees if you happen to get called the wrong one. Amongst the strengths of Women of Colour internationally is a long tradition of working with textiles and clay. Merely craft media. Curiously it is possible to identify the influence of these *craftsworks* on *real art* and *real artists* who obviously are eligible for hanging fees. Regardless of the technical skills and knowl-

159

edge necessary to produce *craft* an exhibition of such works is unlikely to raise a hanging fee from the Welsh Arts Council or The Arts Council of Great Britain. The status and hence the income of the *craftsperson* is lower than that of the *artist*. To use cloth is to assume a different role, unless that cloth is canvas stretched on a frame, and then it doesn't matter what the quality of your production is, it is *art* by existing in a particular format. The definition could be summarised thus: anything which the white boys make themselves is *art*. Anything which they can't quite figure out is less, is *craft*.

Several years ago I decided to make and exhibit some prints on paper which unlike prints on cloth are *art* in order to access *artist* status. Last year after five years of professional practice I received my first hanging fee for an exhibition of ceramics and batiks. In the application to the Welsh Arts Council I was described as *sculptor*. Regardless of what I get called *I am the same person*.

An extract from *Crafty Definitions: Name Calling and Money*, an article by Nina Edge first published in Black Board WEMAS. Summer '90.

The interaction of the maker with the material makes the object what it is. What the maker has done with the medium ought to be a reasonable way of finding a name for the resulting object. To date this has not been the case, dubious references to what the maker is already described as, in the culture, pass for an adequate definition for products on sale.

Attempts at basing the 'name' around notions of function are equally muddled. These attempts take as a base line that so-called functional wares, vessels for liquids and solids are craft – definitely *craft*. It does not provide *sculpture* as the logical resting name for clay objects which are not containers, but merely implies that they might not be *proper* craft. Given the long history of pre-industrial ceramics which are not vessels but perhaps function as architectural detail or commemorative objects this is perhaps a little arrogant and ignores the function of objects which are not vessels but perhaps ornaments, perhaps sculptures (for example, Christening cradles made in English Slipware or Staffordshire White figures). The variety in scale and meaning of objects made in the so-called craft media may defy definition. Their name being ultimately less important than their quality and that they should be produced at all in a machine and indeed micro-machine age. What is, unfortunately, of crucial importance to makers is the relationship between definitions and remuneration and hence survival in the culture at all.

An enquiry to The Welsh Arts Council regarding a submission to the slide library is met with an enquiry from The Welsh Arts Council as to which media the maker works in. If the response is clay then the only department willing to house slides of anything made in clay is The Welsh Crafts Council. The result of slides being held in a particular department is that those who refer to the art section are denied the opportunity to know the full range of materials in which art is made in Wales. The maker ends up in the wrong place unless he/she does happen to be making vessels or the type of objects which buyer and seller agrees is craft. The crucial point is that as policy The Welsh Crafts Council does not provide hanging fees for crafts exhibitions, although it does provide hanging fees of £250 for exhibition of *art*. The difficulty which those defined as craft makers experience raising hanging fees, coupled with a policy of pricing work defined as *craft* well below the prices of work defined as *art* makes it look like an act of folly to go within twenty paces of any craft defined media unless money is no object. A possible inclusion to such illogical name calling practices is that only those already enjoying good fortunes need consider making objects by hand (unless they can prove them to be sculptures) or colouring cloth by hand (unless they can prove that cloth to be canvas, and the product not textiles but painting).

This has negative implications for women who are as standard poorer than men. The implications are worse though for black women who, through the practices of racism, enjoy considerably less financial power than their white-skinned sisters. So like it or not, this is the context within which craft practice currently operates in the United Kingdom. Neither arts people nor crafts people can define what craft is in any satisfactory way.

That which appears to be crafts practice which consciously or sub-consciously is sub-divided into:

(i)   high craft – that which is acknowledged by major funds, curators and marketeers, the craft of graduates;

(ii)   lesser craft – that which forms an area of production heavily reliant on the tourist and nostalgia industry, and

(iii)   invisible craft – that produced by un-named crafts people – piece-workers, at home or in factories.

161

Despite the sludge it is quite obvious that the invisible crafts people are largely women. Their number include many Blackwomen. And whether or not any objects made in materials which have a history of use either in the craft world, or in the range of cultural production, which are traditional female strongholds, can ever be called *art*, and indeed paid for as such, remains to be seen. It is into this mess that Blackwomen practitioners dance if they are involved in making certain types of objects, or if they make objects out of certain materials.

No matter what context their work occupied in the mother culture, if they are in a position to access a mother culture, and no matter how well they might be able to exclusively operate in any of the many Black communities and market places as a small part of the total population, it is within the context of the majority that it will rest as cultural production. Having said this, there is room for development of essentially Black market places as there is for development of all areas of life for Black people, and in particular for Blackwomen in contemporary Britain.

The speed of development will depend on which areas are prioritised by Black people as well as areas which are prioritised for them through the unpredictable and often outrageous behaviour of the majority white population. If the practice of racism in Britain as well as in mainland Europe continues to spurt at its current rate of development, the skills of creatively orientated Black people are likely to be once again diverted into the politics of survival, into the campaign work, and direct interventions. Blackwomen craft workers are in an exacting and exciting position, in terms of their developing abilities to produce objects which include depictions of themselves and their people which are neither eurocentric in their taste nor sexist in their content. The number of women of colour who use their hard-won spending power to buy the work of Black craftswomen is perhaps as inspiring as some of the work itself. In discussing sales outside of Black markets it is as well to be aware of the blight which in world terms has long been the boot in the Black craftworkers face; that of appropriation. The level and degree of male/female appropriation is as nothing to the appropriation of technologies, design work, content and meaning which the colonised world has suffered at the hands of the colonisers. It follows the lines of the appropriation, theft if you like, of major cultural works along with material riches from all over the world. There are as many examples in Music and Mathematics as there are in the Art and the Craft world.

Contemporary small scale craft pottery owes its presence in Britain to its importation from Japan by, then serviceman, Bernard Leach in the

162

'thirties. His enormously influencial book *A Potters Book* contains the technology of small-scale production in Japan and was in many cases the only technical information the first swelling of craft activists in the 'sixties had under their arms when they set out to fulfill their rural dreams. This is almost entertaining given the role which the tourist craft industry knowingly or unknowingly plays in the manufacturing of the idea of an 'all British' Britain. It has to be said, however, that in this appropriation at least the inventors of the technologies are clearly acknowledged and that the event probably did a good deal to promote Japanese/British relations in the post war years. Far more insidious are the incidents of appropriation in which the inventors go un-named, un-acknowledged. This has implications for the constructions of 'history'. Observe the ways ex-colonised peoples are regarded in the countries of the colonisers, and in the ways in which colonised peoples view themselves and hence their own development. It has its effect in, for example, the low numbers of school pupils of colour who regard art or craft practice as being part of their heritage and strength, worthy of serious considerations as a career, worthy of respect.

Linked to the disproportionately small numbers of Black pupils applying for post school level courses in arts subjects is the fact that racism in schools often prevents careers teachers and advice services from considering the arts as a viable course for Black pupils to pursue. Attached to this in turn is a kind of romanticisation of art/crafts practice that causes it to be viewed as a privileged occupation. And needless to say, Black pupils are seldom pointed in the direction of occupations that are seen as being anywhere near 'privileged' in the view of the majority white population. Still it seems another layer of sludge defines the presence of Black people in Britain specifically designed to perform the jobs which are nasty, not to work in fields to which large numbers of white people aspire. Somewhere floating around in this layer is the notion that women came here as dependents and that is the role they should perform. In many many cases careers advice staff are infinitely sexist in their approach to their work. A few have failed to note to their subconscious that Black British women have been born here for hundreds of years and should perhaps not be seen along Home Office 'dependence' guidelines. Un-acknowledged appropriation is one area of perceptual hindrance to young Black people engaging in Craft practice.

Another hindrance, also linked to racism, is a desire not to be associated with practices which by their very place within Western machine/consumer culture are defined and marketed on the grounds that they are 'primitive' technologies. Hence a desire may be expressed to be associ-

163

ated, not with the 'primitive' craft technologies but with the 'sophisti-cated' film and video technologies. The ultimate deterrent is that in most cases Craft is an insecure and difficult occupation to engage in, particu-larly in the first few years of practice. Anyone with responsibilities to feed, clothe and house any people other than themselves will necessarily be discouraged from entering the trade in favour of trades with faster and more reliable financial rewards.

Often in the initial years of practice considerable capital investment is desirable and the poor record of financial institutions in terms of their willingness to lend money to Black people is a further example of the ways in which institutional racism prevents certain activists from reaching anything near their full potential. So appropriation has a far reaching effect in terms of the way in which potential Black artists see themselves, and in how those enjoying positions of power perceive Black artists during all stages of their development. All areas of production of artifacts in Europe have always been highly 'influenced' by wares which were imported from China, India, Java, Malaysia and many Afrikan countries. So called 'paisley' designs from Orrissa were manufactured in Britain, so called 'dutch wax prints', work derived from Javanese Batiks, were knocked off in Holland and the whole of northern Europe rushed to emulate porcelain like that which had arrived from China. Without exception the quality both of design and materials used in Europe to copy work first seen in its colonies was infinitely inferior to the genuine article. Various devices were employed in attempts to mask the pretenders. Shawls made in imitation of Kashmiri shawls were wrapped in paper previously soaked in patchouli oil, encouraging buyers to believe that the British copies were genuine Indian imports. At the same time the means of production in the countries of their inventors were systemati-cally destroyed. Part of the legacy of this practice is the association of Black craftspeople with inferior quality goods, which in actual fact were only ever copies of goods made by the master and mistress craftspeople in the colonised lands. In contemporary times Imperialism allows the importation of beautifully made products from a range of countries whose economies, reeling in the after-blow of colonialism, have to be grateful for any hard currency they can raise. In the context of the European market they can be had ridiculously cheaply.

Less than one pound will buy you a hand-carved stone box from India of immense beauty. There is not a craftsperson in Europe (native) capable of producing such skilfully worked ware and if there were I hardly think that they would would be charging less than the price of a pint of beer for it. During the last two summers an array of printed fabrics have appeared as garments all over Britain. It is fantastically beautifully coloured and patterned and, as a result, extremely popular. They are the result not of skilful British design but of skilful British appropriation. They are direct lifts of traditional and modern Javanese batik designs, which having been recorded under the guise of anthropology, are not covered by copyright laws and hence are easy pickings. There is no requirement for designers who so lack the innovatory skills of the Javanese to acknowledge their source. It is impossible to conjour up a reverse equivalent i.e. of designers in Asia needing to rip off British textile designs, but if such a scenario were to take place it would be a very short time before legal proceedings would follow. Instances of such appropriation are so frequent, so widespread, that counter moves seem pointless. This effectively prevents young Black designers from access-ing their own heritage as parts of their design heritage are always being represented to them as European. Within the European frame of produc-tion, design elements are sucked to death to fill the ever hungry belly of the fickle world of fashion. The demands of the consumer culture are that things become passé within a year, so the fashion designers are likely to continue their world appropriation tours, and are likely to continue to fail to name or pay their sources of 'inspiration'. There is a terminal problem amongst the Europeans in their inability to properly acknowl-edge that Black people ever did anything of value on the planet, let alone attain standards of production, skill and artistry beyond the scope of the white cultures.

The all embracing smell of racism which permeates British society prevents many of the more rightful inheritors of art forms from outside Europe by blocking the path of potential Black artists in education. It is often white students who receive travel grants to study textiles in India, or sculpture in Ghana, it being too often assumed that Black students somehow have 'connections' everywhere and would be able to visit their homelands independently. Contrary to this view but used as an argu-ment alongside it, is the idea that, for example, carnival designers trying to raise funds to travel to Trinidad are really just looking for a ticket to visit relations and to party. All too often it is easier for white students to study the art forms of 'other' peoples than it is for their Black counter-parts. Meanwhile in the colleges white students using 'ethnic' sources are praised for their perceptual skills in noticing the quality (and market potential) of such work. They are more likely to gain respect and good grades whilst Black students using 'ethnic' sources are not really seen as doing any work at all, but merely reproducing what they already 'know'. On leaving college the story changes, the goal posts are moved as galleries and buyers demand 'ethnic' looking work at 'ethnic' prices.

165

Outside of the Black market places, in the mainstream world, there is a greater number of buyers, often with more spending power. Their ability to influence the production of Black craftspeople with their cheque books would be hard to measure, but as holders of greater amounts of capital they are in a position to call the tune. Black workers in the craft world have experienced such insulting treatment by the mainstream as to be followed studiously by gallery staff who assume that the presence of Black people 'off limits' implies a security risk. They are also subject to rude and nosey questions about their personal and family histories, and sometimes subject to being treated with contempt if they turn out to be, in the opinion of the questioner, not quite Black enough, not exotic enough, not genuinely 'ethnic'. For example, a reduction in status afforded to Asian craftworkers who do not speak any Asian languages. In most cases this behaviour hits Black British born craftworkers more than those born in the motherlands, or elsewhere in the various diasporas. They are less able to perform the role of international tourist guides and facilitate the type of voyerism which some white cultural workers still believe is their due. Curiosity is a major tool for learning, and questions and exchanges can be rewarding for all people, but there are subtle differences in some interactions where the assumption of roles of power and superiority by white workers affect the confidence and happiness of Black workers.

Having noted the negatives of operating within the mainstream it has to be acknowledged that, like all things in life, the range of experiences is vast, and the importance of selling and showing work in the 'proper culture' cannot be underestimated. Black crafts workers would be sadly diminished in their power if they politely took themselves off to their own ghetto. This brings us to the question of spiritual well-being because survival in this department can be more fraught when we venture beyond areas in life which have been marked out for us. Participation in mainstream activities and organisations can be dangerous and seem to be more trouble than they are worth, more damaging than they are useful. A balance is sometimes hard to achieve, between operating in spiritually supportive environments and sorties into the mainstream. There is much to be learned in both areas, which may become more separate, and may become more fused, it will doubtless be interesting sniffing around in the process of finding out.

In effect working in what are presently seen as two separate areas, the Black Arts world and the mainstream, doubles the workload of a Black practitioner who wishes and/or needs to work in both. The phenome-

166

non of The Black (usually group) Exhibition as being an area designated, designed for and sometimes by Black people is prone to being viewed, in patronising terms by the mainstream. This results in it becoming important to show work in the mainstream regularly to prove the worth of work which otherwise is seen to merely fulfil equal opportunities legislation, as positive discrimination, as tokenism. It is easy for Black workers to become overstretched especially when practitioners also work in the field of education in attempts to counter continuing isolation of Blackwomen students, and the ignorance of their white counterparts. An interesting challenge, or a no-win situation? In terms of the immense satisfaction and development possible in the field of making, in terms of the pure act of making in materials which are beautiful, sensual and simple, and stepping over the sludge, it is possibly less a no-win situation, and more a no-loose gamble.

INGRID POLLARD, "Olive Pollard in her Garden, Autumn 1990"

Olive Pollard

Each Plant I Love

Mrs. Olive Pollard in conversation with her daughter Ingrid Pollard.

Ingrid: *How long have you had a city garden?*

Olive: 29 years, 16 in Nelson Road and nearly 14 in Alexandra
            Road, North London

Ingrid: *Do you spend a lot of time and money on your garden?*

Olive: Yes, I spend around 35 to 40 pounds a year. Also I do a lot
            of propagating and share plants with my neighbours. I
            spend a lot of time now that I'm not working – I'm retired
            – I spend about 8 to 10 hours a week in my garden. When
            I was working just about 4 or 5 hours a week because of
            course during the week you are at work and then at week-
            ends you do your housework and so I couldn't spend as
            much time as I do now.

Ingrid: *Did you garden in Guyana?*

Olive: No. My parents did but I used to look after the houseplants,
            water them, cut the dead things off, leaves and stuff, and
            transplant.

Ingrid: *What sort of gardening did they do?*

Olive: Lots of fruit and vegetables, in Guyana, and exotic flowers,
            things that you can't grow here.

Ingrid: *And what are those things that you can't grow here?*

Olive: Like bougainvillaea and crotons, different kinds of crotons,
            that's in the flower line but the fruit and the vegetables,
            bananas and breadfruit and peppers, different peppers,
            limes and things like that.

Ingrid: *So the gardens were mainly for fruit and vegetables not really
            flowers?*

Olive: That's right, yes.

Ingrid: *What are the favourite plants in your garden?*

Olive: I love the roses. My favourite rose is *Golden Showers* it's beautiful, it's never ending with blooms. Of my plants and trees, my sumac are beautiful.

Ingrid: *Do you make trips to flower shows or Kew Gardens, if so do you go along with friends or alone?*

Olive: I used to when I was working, I used to go with friends because where I used to work we always had coach tours all through the summer to Chelsea and other Flower Shows. All ladies trips, we used to go together but now that I'm on my own, retired, I go but not as often. I belong to the National Rose Society and I go to the gardens during the summer months.

Ingrid: *Did you ever enter any competitions?*

Olive: Not like Chelsea, those shows, but I enter competitions for flower arranging. Different places like church, when they have church exhibitions. When they have shows there I enter them and I've got a few certificates.

Ingrid: *Do you feel that gardening is an art form?*

Olive: Yes, because you express yourself. I express my feelings with my flower arranging and even in the garden. The colours and things like that you do, that's how I express my feelings, so for me it is an art form.

Ingrid: *Sometimes when you make flower arrangements you have to interpret different stories?*

Olive: Yes, once we had to do nursery rhymes in the demonstrations. I did *Alice in Wonderland* and I did *Snow White and the Seven Dwarfs*, so you have to express a story, how you see them.

Ingrid: *Are you a member of any gardening society or groups?*

Olive: Yes, when I was working it was the Standard Telephone and Cable's Womens' Flower Class and I also belonged to the Royal National Rose Society.

Ingrid: *Could you tell me what your garden means to you?*

Olive: It means everything to me, I love my garden. Each plant I love them like if they were my children.

Patricia St. Hilaire **Seven Poems**

NANNY

Nanny is an old black West Indian woman living in 1986, she is sixty two years lived, 5' 5" tall, and about fifteen stones in 100% solid woman.

Her face is as dark as the inner shell of the nutmeg, lighter in some parts too, just like the shell, smooth in places and slightly lined in others.

Eyes that are special for they tell a story that has no end or beginning. These eyes have seen all, and as you shift in the light yet another story is told. Her eyes are the shape of a full almond, the colour brown and smooth, pupils appear to be navy blue with a hint of white around the edge shaped like a thin half moon.

Her eyes dip down towards her nose like a fish about to turn. A nose so like my mother's, so on its own, it's just like no other, you see the sides go up and out as if in courtesy and bow, and cheekbones high and fleshy, they tell you when she's happy or sad, such a movement in her face, a language of its own, and one that I know better than that from the tongue.

Lips that are full and plenty with my dimple just above the top lip that moves so swiftly . . .

She has a lovely body that has no age to see, shapely and voluptuous and every inch a woman, age does not come into play, she is a fine black woman, fine indeed and I love her ever more, her logic, her being, she is all I dream of in being and having in my nanny.

October 1986

TREE LIKE WOMAN

I saw a woman tall and dark - standing amidst the trees,
Tall and thin,
Thin and straight,
She stood with her head arched back
With her face to the sky
Clear to the sky
Her arms stretched up and out,
Out, pointing towards the sky,
Long limbs clear to the sky,
Palms facing,
Arms reaching,
Up and up and up,
Up the side of her face, her ears, reaching and reaching

She saw no-one watching her as she stood rooted, growing,
Reaching, soaring, as her tree-like-self took root.
She saw no-one pointing at her, as her nakedness was
Seen,
She heard no-one calling her, as her hair flew free in
the air.
Her ears were full of the howling of the wind not crying,
But singing a special song.
She felt nothing as they tried to cover her body and all
her nakedness.

Her feet could not be seen,
They tried to find them, digging, faster and faster but
no,
No feet were to be found, for she was truly rooted deep
into the earth with all her might, she was rooted . . . . .

There were screams of horror,
How could this be a woman rooted like a tree?
Rooted like a tree, a tree, a tree . . . . . ?
People wanted not to know, not to remember what they had
seen
A horror to them is what they thought they had seen,
When in fact what they did see was a woman at source with
her Soul,
With her centre, with the woman in herself . . . . .

'twas nothing unreal, but they had begun to faint,
'twas nothing unreal for this woman,
was one of the same . . . . .
The trees were calling, wailing and howling,
The people began to run, or at least try to . . . . .
Then there was a silence, a stillness . . . . .
The skies opened up and the rain began to fall and as it
did,
So did the leaves from all the trees,
Soon there were no leaves on any of the trees . .
And the tall, thin, tall and straight,
Straight and dark woman,
Stood well proud,
For she had joined the tall dark trees of the forest,
Who reached clear to the sky with beauty . . . . .

1986

PURPLE TWISTED GINGER

The woman cried
Red purple tears
They trickled down her face
Hot molten
Red purple tears
Burnt her
As she released them

Her raw veins
Were naked
Barefaced, green
Barley blue
Red
They ran dry

They smoked
And scorched
They curled up
And died
Her veins

A deep red hole
Lively, bubbling flesh
Hot torn flesh
Red and white veins
Open arteries
Endless tunnels
To places unknown

The woman bleeds
From within her walls
I saw twisted fingers
The smell of ginger root
Burning
Twisted, contorted fingers
Fingers, ginger
Ginger fingers
What did I see?

Fingers and arms
Like a reflector
Of twisted metal
Skin like smooth
Ginger root
Golden too

Fingers dug into
The woman
Like metal
Holding herself
Comforting herself
Hurting herself

We saw the woman
Her tears
Her bones
But most of all
We saw her
Naked pride

April 1988

PYEYUCCA

As I lay holding the pillow
That I wished could have been Pyeyucca
I despise that part of me
That has me laying in bed at this time
But I have to and I must . . .
When I am the mistress of the soul
That I drink and dance with
How can I take flight into the tender blackness of night
That blackness that is as mellow
As the ivory keys that play
Those mellow mourns.

See my body
You may never have opened your eyes
For in your mind
You have a painted image
Am I a panther?
A puma?
Am I agile, long and swift?
Keep your thoughts, they are yours.

I am lying on white sheets
Holding the pillow that didn't leave
Once the ivory keys stop playing
There are no longer tears
No, I feel very little
For I have long got used to that stranger
Who visits that part of me
That I care not to feel
Sometimes I wonder how I would feel
if I were Pyeyucca

Or the prostitute and the actress
Both half-clothed and swaying
To the ebony and ivory keys

The actress singing a song
Or playing the flute
The prostitute dancing to the sound
Of a blackman's laughter
The sound of tossing coins
Ringing in both their ears . . .
Two different plays
The same person and two different places . . .
But - are they?
Passionate gaze they hold for each other
They are lovers
They hold no false smiling faces
Together in the same mind are they
But are they the prostitute and
Or the actress?

Cool soft black rounded body
Lay between white sheets
Holding comfort encased in white
Long black arms holding this white piece
Of comfort like a mother holding the unborn child
Bended knees to stop and protect it refusing it
Entry into . . . into . . . into . . .

She falls into the place she would ideally like to be
Her skin as black as jet with
Dew drops from the early morning dawn
That carries a scent
As sweet as the petal of the fuchsia flower
Her partner lies close by
There is no dead scent no dead flowers
In this rare moment no tension
Just a reach for each other's limbs
A word of worship sent out in their
Eyes keeping holding the memory of
Their loving for each other
With a breath of air she/we/they
Give each other the sign of . . . of . . . of . . .

Birds are singing soft and tranquil
Soft and
        soft and . . . . .
                    soft . . . . .
                            and . . . . .

FOUR TALL WALLS

The woman said,
I want you to take responsibility for putting her here,
It is you who should feel the cold,
the way that she does . . . . .
who hates the sun as she does
the parks as she does
who cannot bear the smell of cologne,
who cannot look at or touch a bristled chin,
who never sleeps on her back,
never has flannel striped sheets,
who never has lace net curtains at her bedroom window,
who could never have a blue painted door . . . . .
who never listens to the radio in bed,
who always sleeps with a candle light . . . . .

You are responsible . . . . .

In her silence these things make her,
hold her back,
her head,
her belly,
that stops her feeling life
prevents her female,
that keeps her within these four white walls,
she thinks that she is thin,
prays to be ugly,
fat,
shapeless,
unattractive,
not feminine,
she covers her body . . . . .

She wants all these things so that you,
and others like you will leave her alone . . . . .
so that her six year old body can grow up in peace,
without being forced ripped,
without your force ripping her six year old body . . . . .

You are responsible for her being here . . . . .
within these four white tall walls . . . . .

THE MEMORIES THAT REMAIN

35, No. 35 Norcott Road
An old small house,
Small, Dark
Shallow in depth
Sharp edges

Dark wood
Doors, shelves, window frames
All painted white

Painted white to bring
Light to this dark house

Wall cupboards
Under stairs cupboards
Hiding places
Secret places

Cold, dark, dank, damp
Smelly spaces
Wet damp walls
Cracked walls
Broken shelves
Escape

Frail, boney, skinny
            girl
Dark and Stringy
Scared, alone, waiting

Crying, hiding
Burning
Hot Tempered
Uncontrolable,
Deadly thoughts
Untouchable

Small hands reaching
Round eyes begging
Throbbing heart beat
Small feet . . . . .
            Stuck
Panting, panting

Back bent sharp
Knees brittle
Eyes dry - blood cold

No voice escapes her
Yet action of beckoning
Move
     Move
          Moves her

Don't come close
She'll make you know

Don't come close
she moves away
Don't come close
She'll see you
Don't come close
She'll hear you

Don't care for me
She'll beat me
Don't
     Don't . . . . .

She runs into
The dark, dank
Dark, dank space
Under the stairs
She's safe
       She's safe

No one can save her
No one can see her
This frail, boney, skinny girl
This frightened fearful stringy girl

Scared, alone, waiting
Just waiting
To crumble like the walls around her

Dark, dank, damp, smelly walls

1966, in No. 35, a nightmare began

1967, it grew a little more
Darker and deeper
The scars grew worse

1988, the scars still in view
She has the only view
Memories of the past

A crazy sounding woman
Laughing
Laughing
Only rarely did she do much else
Then when she did
She cried
This crazy sounding women

Scars that hold memories
Of nightmares dear
That equal no weight in gold
She has them well hidden

Yesterday she found a key
Silver wrapped in gold
It said in short
It's time
It's time
To use me
          Now

Today she sits alone
Awaiting the right time - to open the door

And welcome in her past
Her ghost
Her source
Her memory

And the crazy sounding woman

"I wouldn't want to return here"

When it's my time
My time to die
I want you all to cry
and feel as you will.
But at the end of that time,
I want you all to enjoy
The good times with a smile
And the sad times as you will.

I don't want to live to be old,
and already, sometimes I feel old . . . . .
I would really like to stop,
and start all over again now.
So that I could end this pained life,
that has so many ill memories . . . . .

If I die young
what ever age that is,
remember, it gives me another chance,
to stop the hurts and sadness that so few of you know . . . . .
or could see in me,
my life . . . . .
I want you all to celebrate,
and miss the things you liked about me,
and be glad that I am not here to upset you anymore . . . . .
with all the things you didn't like about me . . . . .

I have not always enjoyed being here,
so for those times I'll be glad to go,
but for all of you who I leave behind,
I'll only miss you for a while . . . . .
for I shall always be a part of your life
both past and present . . . . .
always in the present . . . . .

So when I die,
think of me resting
(as so many of you already tell me to)
I shall be resting and healing my wounds,
I know not how long that process will take,
for the wounds I bear are deep . . . . .

I remember thinking to myself,
What lesson was there to learn?
As yet do not know
I don't believe that I could bear another
life time here . . . . .

I wouldn't want to return to this place.

But if I do I should like to be the wind,
the aïr, that you'll breathe
the breath that is life itself

For that will always be life at its best . . . . .

June 2nd 1988

CLAUDETTE JOHNSON: *Pushing Back The Boundaries*, invite, 1990

Frederica Brooks

Ancestral Links: The Art of Claudette Johnson

I know about how and where the feculence of this system manifests itself in making life/creativity a battle for Blackwomen, especially; but at the moment I don't feel like dirtying my brain, theoretically articulating any of it. I just need to take time out to simply start up a dialogue by acknowledging the creativity of one of the many Blackwomen artists out there working.

Claudette Johnson uses pastels and gouache thoroughly worked. 'Portraiture' is an inept term for describing her work, though she does make images of people – Black women. Single figures – sometimes two or three – life sized and larger, take up the whole of the picture space, leaving no room for backgrounds to detract from her central concern. Claudette is defiant of the portrait's restrictive western associations – not simply in that her women are black – but because she depicts them dancing, flirting, oozing eroticism, masturbating, menstruating, and tumbling around their picture space. Sensually round bottoms are held high. The women also show insecurities at times, have moments of quiet, or stand brashly – hands on hips – cutting dem y'eye pan you. Her work is rarely titled, which makes it difficult not to examine it as a whole body. I do however see three main means of expression in the work she was doing before 1989, that have come out of particular resources/lack of resources, and experiences: demonstrated by a shift from black and white charcoal drawing of figures, to a form of abstraction, and finally a return to working more figuratively.

Before following the established route of higher art education in 1979, Claudette embarked on 'secret' work dealing with her identity as a black woman. At home, she was making self-portraits. As a consequence of finding it hard to look at herself, the work focussed on aspects which she did not like. She was however, also making very romantic images of blackwomen, as well as the more cathartic pieces. At this time, she was reading works by 1960's Black activists like Rap Brown, James Baldwin, Malcolm X and had reached a state of consciousness where she felt it her right to be identified as an African, given that *'Black'* is such a 'landless' title. It was important to her that artists should be clear about the political position from which they worked or explored.

183

At art college, Claudette found a lack of resources relevant to her work. With no black models to make studies from, she started drawing herself, and going as far as bringing black women she knew into college to pose. She spent a lot of time exploiting the very limited library resources for black women's imagery. In these charcoal drawings, the figures are highly worked with very soft shading. One of the pieces is of an unclothed woman, viewed from behind, lean and athletic. Her weight is shifted onto one leg, her spine curved in compensation. She holds her arms out from her body as if dancing. I was quite taken by her near sexlessness and her look of agility, on top of that, her rich shining skin described by the soft contrasting shading of black on white. Her left hand is faded into the paper, as is her right foot, yet there is power in their absence. The woman is stripped of reference to time and place; no exotic landscape surrounds her. The small ankle bracelet she wears, pertains more to a cosmetic teasing, than to 'traditional ornamentation'.

Another of Claudette's women faces forward – only her right side is drawn, though minus her right arm. Her left hand rests on a left hip suggested by two lines. She stares out glassy eyed with her right eye – the left remains a disturbing white ball in a socket.

Claudette Johnson's progression towards a form of abstraction was encouraged while a student, by her college's abstract-expressionist bias. She did, however, feel she had not been restricted or pushed into that particular way of working as she liked quite a lot of this style of work. She still felt strongly about figurative work, or at least 'work that took the figure as its starting point'. The richly coloured pieces that came out of that period continue her style of not drawing the whole of the figure, by both using the edge of the paper to cut off unwanted parts, and by leaving areas white. In the previous charcoal pieces, the women seem to be stepping out from a white cloud – an undistracting void, against which they perform. In these works the women perform more indulgently, the white areas are treated more positively and perform with, and as part of the women.

A naked, gloriously brown, and rounded, woman takes up the picture space, by hitching the shin of her bent right leg up against the edge of the painting. She spreads her other large brown thigh out towards us, exposing a white breast-sized circle between her legs. Her half-white head nestles into the top corner of the space. With a malignant white eyeball, she sneers, open mouthed. Another woman is pictured mid-tumble. Her torso is lightly suggested in the bottom corner, by a broad

184

mouthed smile, and a hand to steady herself. The line representing her back extends upwards into a most pervasive, well worked, brown backside. It dominates the top half of the painting. The coloured areas behind can only echo its form. The buttocks are presented as the vantage point of the undulating landscape of the woman.

One of the concerns Claudette dealt with in her work was menstruation. In doing so she seems to have used more complex imagery: notably in the backgrounds being patterned by harder triangular shapes that accumulate around/diffuse from the woman's body. This woman is again naked, opening her legs wide before us. Her eyes closed, and lips slightly open, make her look beautiful, but vulnerable. Breasts are suggested by a swirling line, and colouring on her white chest. A circular pouch is collaged to the painting between her legs, filled with a brownish-red wool that spills out onto the woman's thigh. A hand is formed out of her other leg, and its fingers dip into the wool. Lines painted the same colour as this wool, outline parts of her body and the surrounding shapes. Incredibly calm in the face of her abdomen being turned inside out; her hand playing in the blood and cupping the shapes of her womb, suggest a kind of satisfaction and fulfilment in spite of the pain. Claudette had been drawn to naturalistic work, so was glad to be free from making that kind of work, even quite relieved that she was able to work in another way.

The more abstract work came from wanting to use a visual language more common to Blackpeople. Particularly, ancestral links can be made with the ancient Egyptians' use of imagery, the indigenous peoples of Africa – past and present (she had seen, and wanted to use Makonde art and sculpture), and also in how the tradition of Orature creatively expresses the fusion of the social, economic and artistic within communities. It is as if Claudette has wanted to move away from the euro-prescribed way of expression, and has seen a type of abstraction as a better way of reflecting the diverse, multilayered experiences she has had. A lot of what she has worked around, remain abstract feelings, largely because traditionally, Blackwomen under colonialism rarely confronted themselves with them positively, if at all. (An example of this is the piece of the woman totally indulgent in enjoying the often teased largeness and roundness of her bottom.) Though she used abstraction as a means of creating a visual language of her own, she felt the 'common message' in her work became 'hidden or obscured by that form of making images'. At the same time, that was the way she wanted to make images – that was what interested her. In allowing herself this freedom, she reveals the dilemma of consolidating the intrinsic politics of her

185

work, with being creative; 'working in an expressive form that felt good'.

In the third genre of her work (produced from around 1981), she returned to painting the women very much more naturalistically. The women also began to meet by sharing the same picture space. They seem to fuse together, a unification of their energies [though physically, they look to be on different planes]. They continue not to be produced as whole figures; being so large as to be cut off by the edge of the picture space, being suggested by lines, or being left out as white background. Claudette continued to explore Blackwomen's sexuality and the myths surrounding it, their fears, strengths and beauty. The individuals she had model for her, permitted an involvement from the beginning. She has said she would have been unable to make the pieces the same had she not known the women.

Again, she rarely painted in a background that would appropriate the women to a particular place or scene. Any sketched lines are descriptive of parts of the image of the women, and not abstractions to complement her. In one piece, Claudette produced three women standing (each in her own space), and put them together as a triptych. They are clothed, as are most of these women. The first stands with hands on hips, staring out askance; the second clasps her hands in front of her abdomen; the third stands legs slightly apart, holding her hands behind her head. She is dressed in black and wearing make-up, seductive. Being put together in this way, they speak to me more of the 'multi-faceted self', (or at least 'tri-faceted'), than of a comparison between three different women.

In another striking image describing the insecurity of a Blackwoman, the artist has painted a woman with a rich dark complexion, wearing a startlingly bright red dress. Her arms are crossed over her chest and nestle under her clothing. Part of one of her forearms is left unpainted, yet is saying something more poignant about loss, helplessness, disability, than the paint could possibly do. My reaction to this piece probably comes from the completely personal experience of seeing my Jamaican mother adopt this very pose; sometimes during times of simmering wrath, or in times of self-reflection, though more often because of this damned cold British weather. For me, the red of this woman's dress fluctuates between representing the searing heat of a temper, and a comforting warmth.

I'm not sure what it is about her work that goes straight for shaking out feelings and inhibitions, so suppressed I never thought existed in me. Perhaps it comes from seeming full, then only knowing my hunger when

186

I'd tasted these images that validate my reactions as a Blackwoman. The women don't chastise or embarrass, they give occasion to participation. Claudette succeeds in making such evocations in Blackwomen especially, largely because the images themselves are of Blackwomen. Though they talk of quite intimate issues, they are not exposés; they take on the stature of icons, without being iconographical.

Claudette has criticised her work for being, at times, the *"acceptable image of black people, a popular image … dreds … shining skins."* Although this was not her intent *'pandered to that way of thinking'*. Her words are an indication of how far reaching and deep rooted a problem this hailed 'multicultural' society has on questions of race. I find it disturbing that she should feel any kind of accountability to the perpetrators of this hypocrisy; especially as she is the creator of work that confounds stereotypical imagery, and commands positive reaction.

While I feel it important to keep up a discourse on the artist's work itself (simply because there has been so little so far), I also feel it is important to relate that on interviewing her, and speaking to other Blackwomen artists, I have found many similarities, both in what they have encountered in their lives prior to them becoming artists, and also in how those experiences have affected their creativity. Claudette was able to squeeze through the system and enjoy it in parts, because of acculturation, and through wanting to get on well in school. These principles did not help her in the long term, when she came to attending an isolating art college institution. Her work provoked limited interest from teaching staff; and then only on a formal level. *"They were interested if they thought something was well drawn, or if they felt it looked like something else that had been done by some other artist – like Picasso."*

A deconstructive comparison, because it seems not only were they effectively saying 'why bother – its already been done by the *greatest* artist of all time'; but also because they were undermining her experience and intelligence in asking fresh questions in her work. She was at one point *" encouraged to go into film making and photography and to leave drawing and sculpture alone"*. This misdirection had nothing to do with any lack of ability on her part. Content in her work was not talked about – though it was relevant because she was trying to get very particular messages across. Even very evocative images of women shouting or menstruating, could only provoke responses that tried to restrain them; the women were acknowledged to be at best, 'bursting out', and at worst 'receding' or 'under attack'.

187

In spite of these negative isolating attitudes, she was obviously determined to gouge out a space for herself at college. There was nothing there to reassure her of her right to be there; so she made those images for herself. I feel that the directness of her work has a lot to do with a 'need' for it to say very specific things to her, simply because she was unable to get assurances to carry on from anywhere else. I also feel because there is a continuous momentum of directness in her work, that she may have wanted to break through the negative reactions. She has said she particularly wanted to have a dialogue with other black women in her work, though not that she 'particularly' wanted to exclude anyone. Black men, white women, white men, were free to view it – but on her terms. And as a 'communicator' she probably found this 'non valuing' of her work more difficult to accept, knowing that the attitudes come from deep rooted prejudices.

Feminists have, not surprisingly, reacted quite favourably to the work of Claudette Johnson, in view of a common way of seeing the 'personal as being political'. In having identified herself as a Black feminist, she has set herself apart from the mainstream movement, obviously aware of its tendency towards racist modes of thinking.

Contemporary artists who work with feminist concerns are linked, as derivatives of the post-modern culture. In the context of the post-modern art movement, it means a legacy of marginalising black artists' work. She is left outside the system, and is having to piece together her own ambiguous position here, before communicating her concerns. White women, however, have been granted a place in their society from which to argue.

Claudette's work has a simplicity/unambiguity which perhaps comes out of her sifting through complex issues. There is also a kind of 'what-have-we-got-to-lose', undefensive, openness about it, taking the knocks of automatically stereotyping gazes. I'd like to compare this with a kind of cool, arrogant detaching abstraction, in the work of feminist artworld icons such as Mary Kelly, Susan Hiller, Barbara Kruger, that points to a defence of something they already have access to.

The written language has been very important in the development of Claudette's work. Though she does not title her pieces, she has always produced written work at the same time as visual imagery. Alice Walker, Audre Lorde and Toni Morrison have influenced her thinking and working. She at one point wanted to visually recreate the reactions she got from reading about some of Toni Morrison's characters.

Her creativity has been tried (tasted/tormented) in the exhibition market, and consequently by racist art critics. *"In fact it's a lot like being a pawn. The exhibitions serve the purpose of the gallery more than it serves your purpose. It's like working a machine you can't really control, whichever way you point it, it shoots back at you."*

The most valuable thing she has got out of exhibiting, was contact with other Blackwomen artists, as in the *Five Black Women At The Africa Centre* curated by Lubaina Himid in 1983. Discussions would start amongst the women exhibiting, at talks, excavating issues around their work and their own histories with regard to it. It was a bringing together of creative black women.

Claudette's current work comes out of a period of freedom from the art market while working and bringing up two young sons. With these new experiences and observations, she continues to make images of black women. The drawings are large, and executed relatively quickly as a loosening up, and as visualisations of the many ideas for more sustained work. They are mainly pastel drawings in reds, browns and greens; just one or two colours are used for the shadows and highlights, which she puts on the paper in smokey clouds. Parts of their bodies are again cut off by the edge of the paper, more significantly the tops of their heads. The women are largely unclothed; one presses against an invisible wall, with her tensed back towards us; another grins and twists her arm up behind her back – giving a two fingered gesture that's accentuated by jarring pink marks radiating from around the hand. Claudette has also drawn the head and shoulders of a woman with arms open wide, but from her expression, she's certainly not to be fraternised with.

In one piece, a woman, pregnant and naked, stretches upwards, unbalanced by the exertion. She could be kneeling or standing – we don't know because she's drawn from above the knees. There is a tension created by the straggling of her pubic hair – it could easily be waters breaking, blood dripping – the event of a birth.

Generally there is an unfurling of their bodies, described by the stretched poses, and the endurance obviously needed to sustain them. The contorting is similar to that in her previous abstract pieces, only these women are more real, and given more tenacity because of their muscular capabilities. Within this dynamism, the women seem incredibly rooted in their space even without descriptive background lines.

What I find most striking about Claudette's new work, is the prudence reflected in the women's poses and in the brevity of how they are drawn.

This conciseness of the work presents a learning experience shown by the pieces being less giving; in comparison to the cajoling of earlier work. When I interviewed the artist in 1988, during time spent away from exhibiting, she spoke of becoming angry about things, and wanting to express some of that. In a more sustained piece she was working on, of a seated pregnant woman in a lilac top, I was intrigued to see writing amongst the areas of background marks; especially as written work has always been intrinsic to her creative development. By bringing together different kinds of communication, she is continuing to look for an accessible visual language that *"feels good"*.

* All quotes are by Claudette Johnson – taken from an interview with Frederica Brooks (10.9.88). Extracts from the dissertation have been re-edited specifically for this publication.

CLAUDETTE JOHNSON: *Pushing Back The Boundaries* is available from UFP, price £5 with free p & p.

Section Three

Portfolios

The ten portfolios presented here glimpse the range of medium employed by Blackwomen artists; collage, photography, paint, clay, image, text.

The breadth of our concerns are also represented. The politics of location, the representation of Blackwomen and the uses to which art works can be put with regard to our liberation struggles.

Bhajan Hunjan is a printmaker based in Reading, Berkshire; **Sherlee Mitchell** a photographer based in London; **Robyn Kahukiwa** an artist based in Aotearoa (New Zealand); **Sutapa Biswas** an artist based in London as is **Janet Caron** and **Val Brown**. Roshini **Kempadoo** is a photographer based in Leicester; **Jeanne Moutoussamy-Ashe** a photographer and photo-historian based in New York State and **Nina Edge** an artist who uses clay and batik is based in Cardiff, Wales. **Lubaina Himid** and **Maud Sulter** are both artists, teachers and curators based in Hebden Bridge.

191

"View Within", Lithograph

Bhajan Hunjan

Bhajan Hunjan was born in 1956 in Kenya. She studied Fine Art at the University of Reading and the Slade. She has exhibited extensively in recent years in London and the South of England, and in 1989 in New Delhi, India, sponsored by the British Council. In 1989 there were solo exhibitions of her work at the Horizon Gallery, London and Aspex Gallery, Portsmouth.

"Pattern acts as a mirror, an enclosure, a window or a view within. It is a form which has an extensive structure and yet has its limitations.

There are very few positive images of South Asian women around. When I work with images of women it's almost like re-examining my attitudes. I re-address the issues. The issues that one is trying to think about relate to one's background and the present.

Women of my mother's generation did not have the choices that I have. One's thoughts are like a pendulum which swings between the two extremes of having the choice and not having the choice."

Bhajan Hunjan

p.194 "In the Midst...", lithograph

Untitled, The Gambia, 1990

Sherlee Mitchell

These still lifes were taken by the photographer during a visit to the West Coast of Africa. They are inhabited by an integrity and sensitivity which challenges the standard conventions of documentary photography on location.

Untitled, The Gambia, 1990

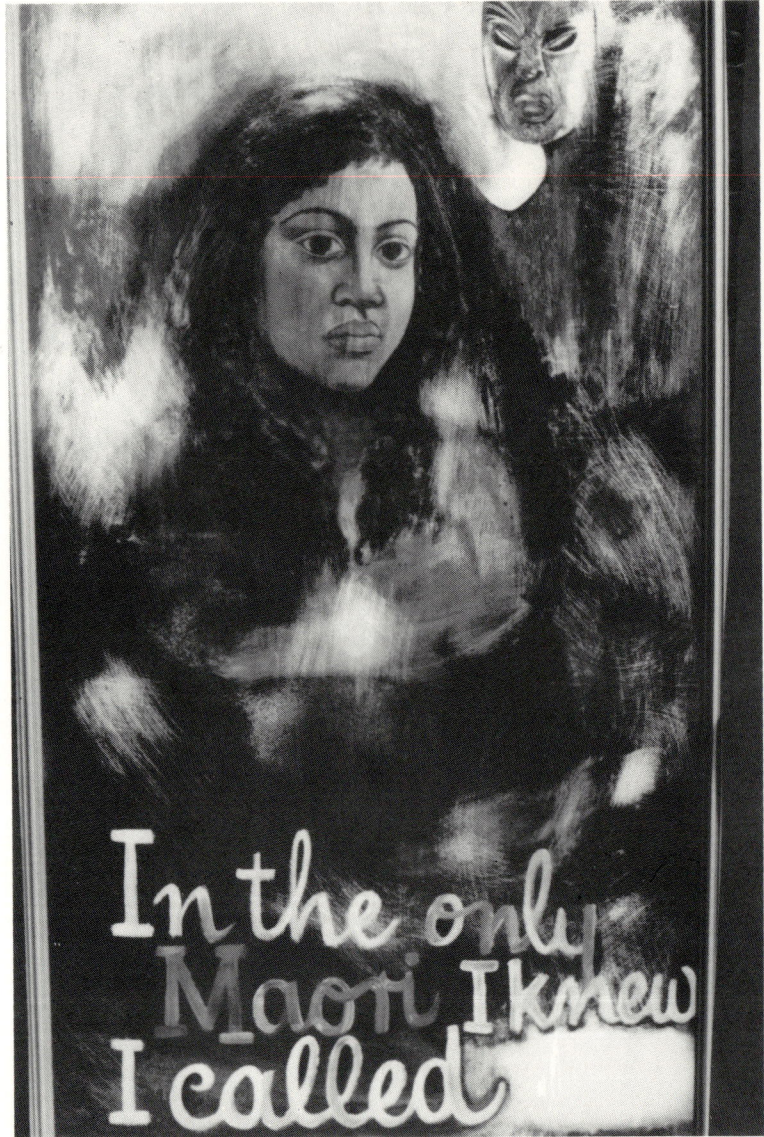

"Tihei Mauri Ora" (I Live), oil on board, 1984

Robyn Kahukiwa

WHAKAMAMAE

Literally translated Whakamamae means, 'to be made to feel pain'.

Robyn experienced the same metaphysical process as she painted HINE-MATIORO. Because of the extraordinary mana of this ariki tapairu of Ngati Porou, Robyn felt unable to portray her until the spiritual climate was favourable. First there had to be a mandate, a commission and permission from the people. This came. Then a series of omens, indications that it was appropriate to proceed with the image of Hinematioro. Robyn remained diffident until Hinematioro began to emerge from her brush. Like Shona, Robyn became a working medium, making guided decisions, incorporating traditional stories about her subject. Both artists have not the least doubt that their work has emerged from the wairau dimension of their Maoriness. Both feel accountable to their tipuna and to their living descendants, he iwi Maori.

Because of the tapu nature of this work, its history, its conception and execution, it has followed that it should be shown in an appropriate ambience. This is why the internal architecture of the gallery has been changed. A wharewhakairo has been created. Just as the ancient Maori artists orginally displayed their work in the external ornamentation of buildings finally evolving into the carved houses of Te Puawaitanga (the classic period), these contemporary artists have chosen to continue that tradition by altering the exhibition space to create one that is essentially Maori. In accordance with that people are required to remove their shoes to protect the delicate whariki on the floor and symbolise their respect for the mana of the house and the work within it. This work expresses the recent history of the Maori and follows through the work of those ancient artists in wood and stone.

"He Aroha Whaereere"

Robyn has continued to explore her Ngati Poroutanga. Her oil pastel drawings on black paper are a new medium for her. It has been a particularly successful one for depicting the power and the ihi of the karanga. The abstraction of traditional carved figures still facinates Robyn. As she becomes more confident in her developing understanding of the intentions of the old artists she is able to include her own ideas about their further development in paint. There are many examples of the movement away from the restriction of wood in this exhibition.

To say that this exhibition has a subversive quality (a criticism which has been levelled at the writing of Patricia Grace) would not be true. These works are open statements which are frankly intended to describe the current state of a formerly sovereign people. They have their roots in anguish and are the creative response to a deep pain which both artists share equally. There is a challenge to non-Maori who see this work to absorb it and to investigate the true history of Aotearoa. In the light of that knowledge lies the responsibility to come to terms with the past in order to create a future in which the tangata whenua can have an equal share in all the good things which this country has to offer.

Quote: 'Report from Havana; Cuba Conversation'.
Art in America, March 1987

na Irihapeti Ramsden

Whakamamae was the title of a two woman show by Robyn Kahukiwa and Shona Rapira Davies. Each artist showed paintings and an installation respectively. Held at the Wellington City Art Gallery in 1988.

"Te Whenua, Te Whenua Engari Kaore He Turangawaewae"
(The Land, The Land but Nowhere to Stand)

"Infestations of the Aorta – Shrine to a Distant Relative", 1989

Sutapa Biswas

Of memory, we change
From one conversation to the next
Always in search of
the edge of the surface
And of textures
There is pleasure
and sometimes none
So thinking back to our space
Marked only by fallen clay
There is both absence and presence

Of violated territories –

You, whose spirit is dull
Brought me here
To the great mountain
Whereupon, I died in the thinness of its air
From violated territories
Its boundaries,
With fierce eyes
I watch
This sacred space.

Sutapa Biswas, 1990

Installation at The Photographer's Gallery, London – Lithofilm
transparencies, and black and white photograph.

"Moon Goddess", stoneware clay, 1987

Janet Caron

"Clay is such an ancient, basic medium to work with. It is used in many different cultures around the world. I feel a common bond with my fellow artists. I too know the feel of clay in my hands. The trepidation as you commit your work to the fire. The excitement, how will it turn out in the end? I want to develop my ceramics to rediscover basic themes, such as: the sun, moon, the seasons and the human form."

Janet Caron came to Britain from Guyana with her parents and sister, Ingrid Pollard (now a renowned photographer) in the late '50s and has lived in London since her arrival. She works in clay and paint.

Since 1988 her work has been exhibited in **The Black Art Festival** in Tottenham, **5 Local Women Artists** at Crouch End Recreation Centre and Ormond Road Workshops. She participated in a ceramic mural project with children at Charteris Community Centre in Finsbury Park in 1989.

"Moon Goddess" by Janet Caron has been reproduced as The Elbow Room Art Card No. 1.

Val Brown

8: 20
t: Austin Cooper
: From Christmas to Christmas May Empire
e Increase
Caption: A Happy New Year to the Empire
layed: December 1927
er: Waterlow and Sons Ltd., London
60 ins. × 40 ins.
(ref: R3
nf: CO 956/311

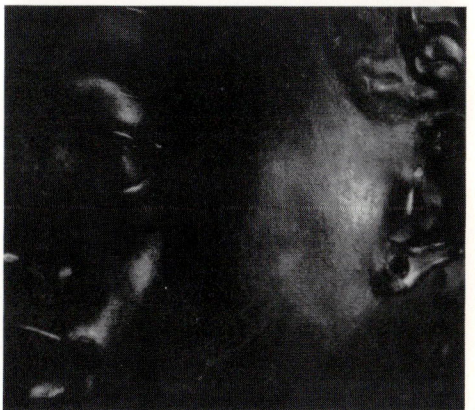

"Head of a Negress" (Colour Photographs)

p.206	1	p.207	4
	2		5
	3		6

Roshini Kempadoo

IDENTITY IN PRODUCTION

"Every self-portrait is inevitably, by its very nature, a doubling, an image of the other."

Jean-Francois Chevrier. 'The Image of the Other'. *Staging the Self* catalogue 1986.

In the creation of the self-portrait, belief in the truth of the self and the objectivity of the photographic record disappear simultaneously. It is the creation of the other, the imaginary distortion, playing the game around identity, the form and fiction of identity that I am concerned with here.

Souvenirs and trinkets

Photography has invariably been a medium used by myself and other Black practitioners living in Britain, to establish, create, form new identities, new images of ourselves. Self-portraiture becomes a means of self-projection, creating an image that presents the self in its own terms, as I would like to be seen, as I would like to affect others. Historically, we have always been subjected, looked at, exoticised and in taking control of the camera, it becomes an assertion of the right to value our own capacities of observation and judgement.

The six pieces I have produced for this exhibition are all these things and more. They are not an effort on my behalf to come to terms with my true self – there is no such thing. They are dealing and raising issues of perception of the self within specific social remits. I make use of my situation, my social and cultural issues, such as multiracial relationships, cultural signifiers as dress, categories of ethnic make-up etc. The use of text with the images acts to contextualise, give authority to or raise complementary issues to the photographs. The photographs are not working on single interpretations and fixed meanings, but aim for multiples of suggestion and comment.

Roshini Kempadoo, 1990

or cultural codings.

Text Credits

p.208 and p.209 'Choosing the Margin as a Space of Radical Openess' by Bell Hooks Framework No. 36 (1989).
p.210 'Black Skin, White Mask', Franz Fanon, Pluto Press (1986)

Roshini Kempadoo produced 'Identity in Production' for *Autoportraits*. An AUTOGRAPH touring show which can be hired from Unit 223, Bon Marche Buildings, 444 Brixton Road, London SW9 8EJ.

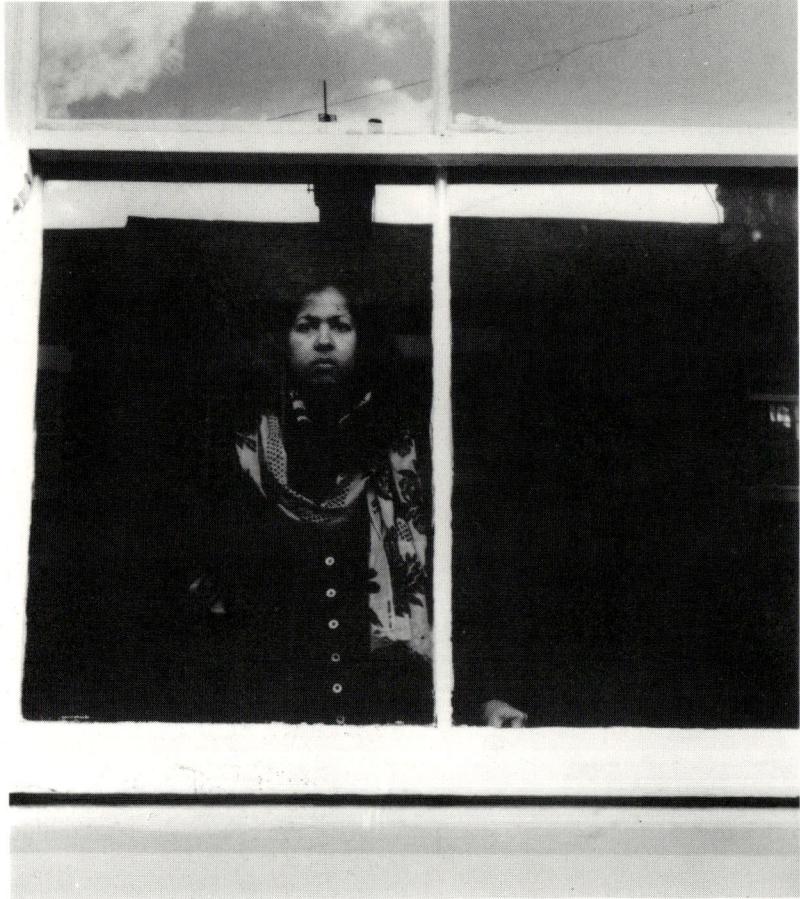

Spaces can be real and imagined. Spaces can tell stories and unfold histories. Spaces can be interrupted, appropriated and transformed.

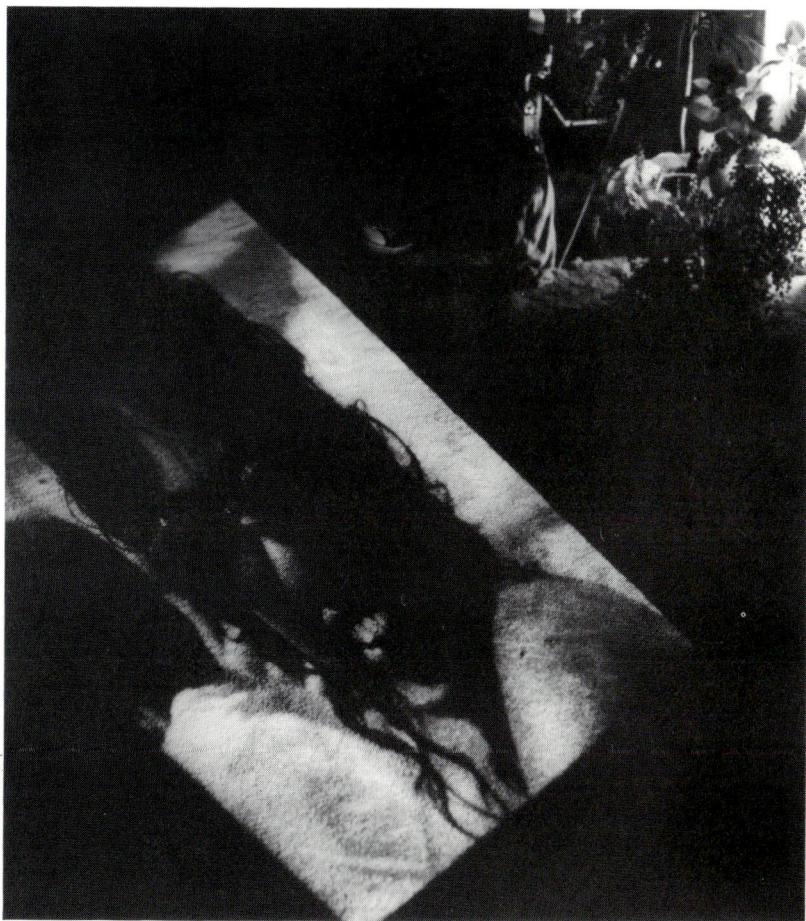

A sense of place, of not just who I am in the present but
where I am coming from, the multiple voices within me.

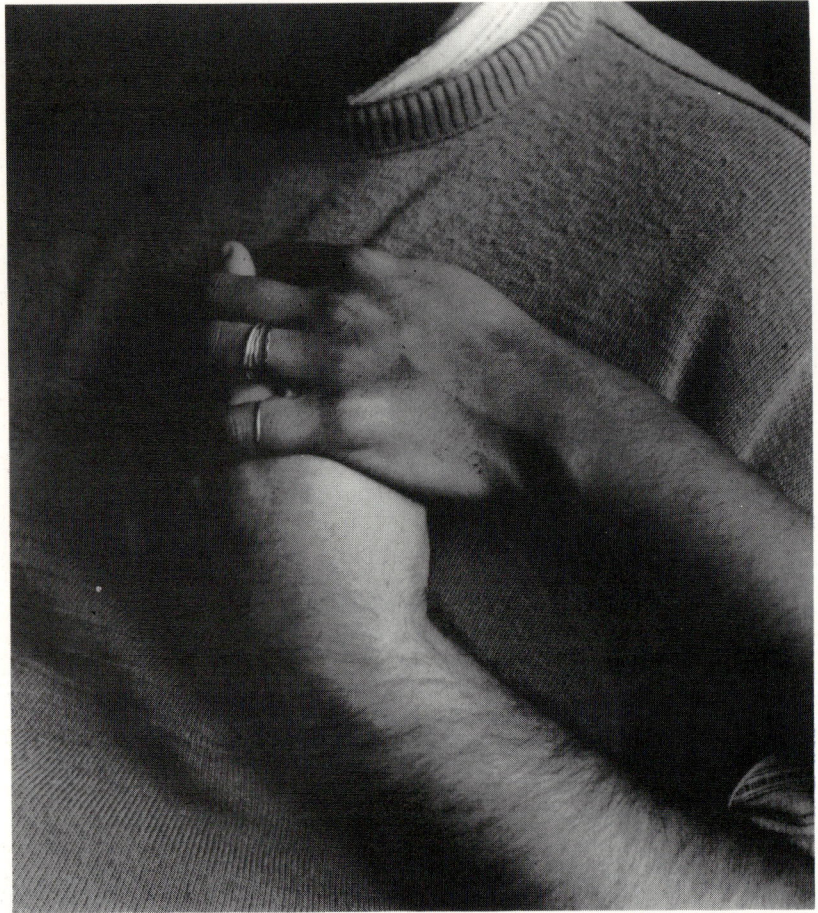

She will not allow herself to see her lover's colour so that
she can concentrate her attention on his devotion.

Who do they expect me to be today.

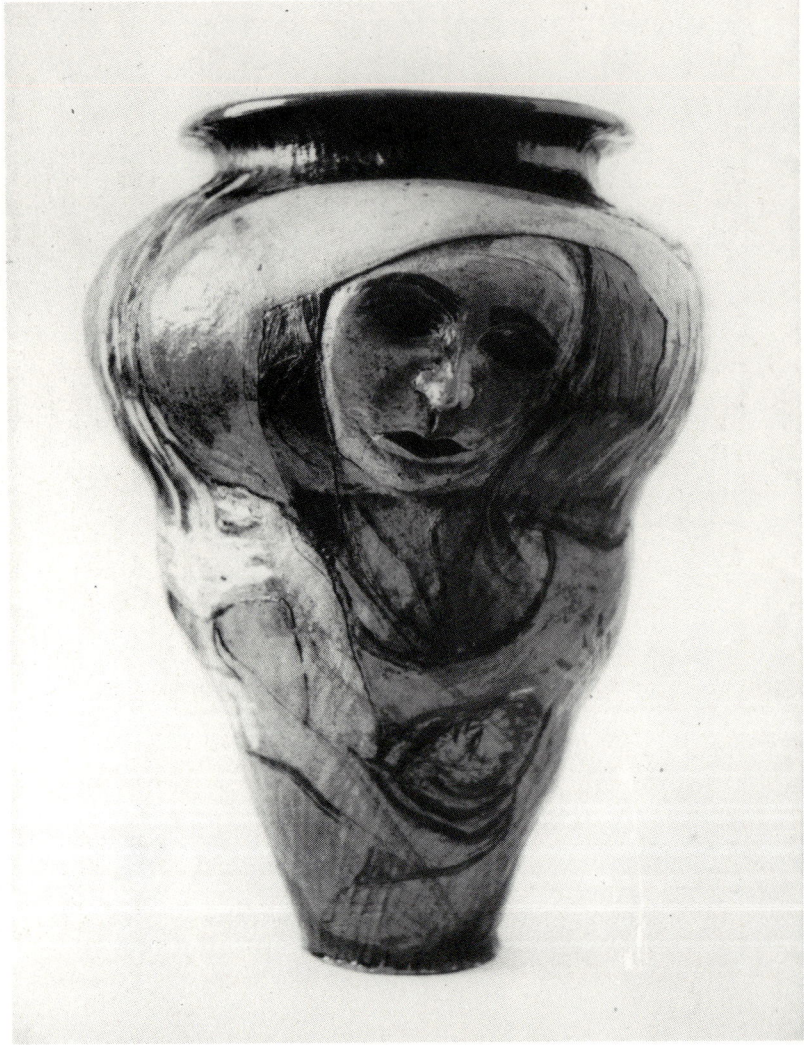

Clay pots

Nina Edge

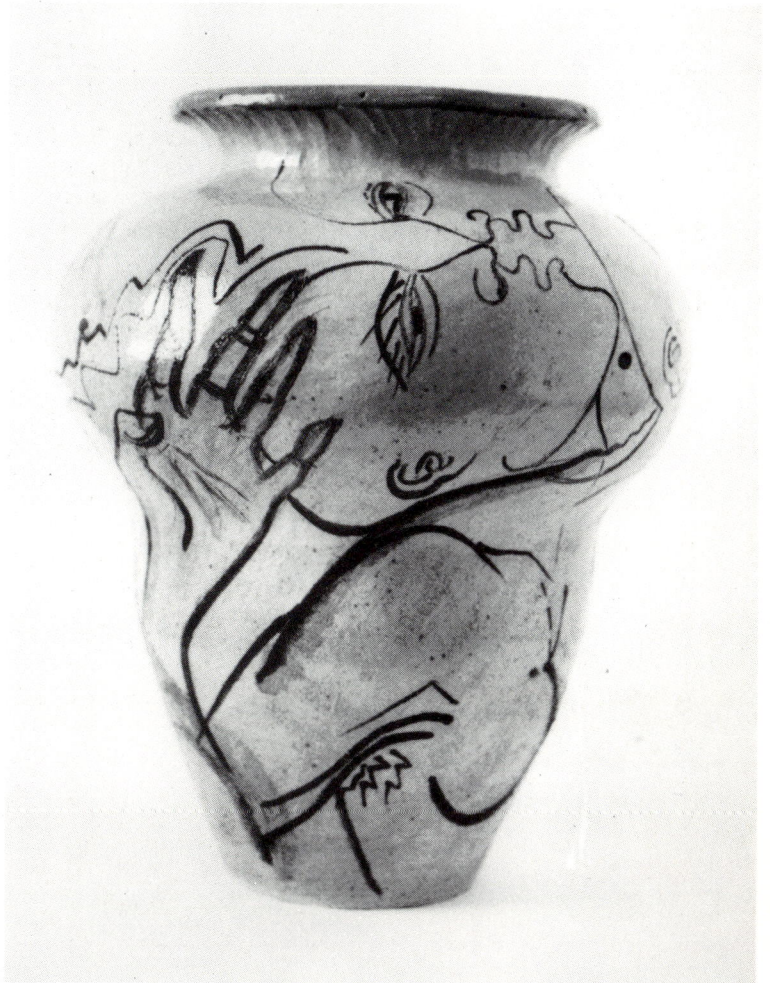

Clay pots

Jeanne Moutoussamy-Ashe

"A photograph captures a piece of time and space. Its essence goes beyond the written word. It offers us an accurate account and gives testimony to what exists within its frame. It bears witness to what occurred in our civilization and time. To photograph is to experience, but to look at photographs is a journey. I would like to take you on a journey to an island where the fight for survival in the midst of progress has come to an end. Its purity and strength has been the beauty of its existence. To experience her people and her land will soon be a thing of the past.

The South Carolina and Georgia Sea Islands bear testimony to America's sophisticates, and they play host to many who go there to experience nature in supreme comfort and relaxation. Hilton Head Island is probably the most well-known of the Sea Islands. One of these dots of land is called Daufuskie island. It is approximately three miles wide and nine miles long. Though it is very near the Georgia coast it is actually within the South Carolina county of Beaufort; Hilton Head Island and Savannah, Georgia are its closest neighbors. Each of these two cities is a forty-five minute ferry boat ride or a twenty-five minute speed boat ride away. Daufuskie itself is rich in history.

In the late 1700's Daufuskie was inhabited by Tory immigrants from England, while her neighbor Hilton Head hosted the True Whigs. The two islands were constantly at war. Daufuskie to this day holds such land titles as Bloody Point and Skull Creek. But Daufuskie and Hilton Head were soon to see wonderfully prosperous times because of their natural resources. They were best known for their Sea Island cotton, its fishing industries, and its low country farming soil. Because of the fighting the islands became mere stopping points for most white visitors, and blacks who had been slaves among the European explorers built comfortable homes.

The American Civil War brought change to Daufuskie and Hilton Head. The Union general in charge of the final devastation of the South limited the sale of all Sea Islands to blacks only. Loyal white northerners who had already bought property in this restricted area were allowed to continue ownership, but no new sales to whites were permitted. Land was sold in small 10- and 20-acre plots that blacks could afford. It was believed that carving up the large plantations would make it more difficult for the Confederates to reclaim their holdings when the war was over. At the war's end the islands became quiet again.

216

Daufuskie Island, "Blossum"

"Man In Front of Church"

The now famous long stapled Sea Island cotton was still growing on Hilton Head at the beginning of the 20th century, and demand increased with World War I. New planters came to the islands in these war years but many became bankrupt with the onset of the Great Depression. The long stapled cotton was soon gone, and the last of the seeds destroyed by the dreaded boll weevil. There were no longer any glittering get-rich-quick-from-cotton promises to lure new planters to the Carolina-Georgia coast. Fishing took its place as the number one industry.

The Depression also forced many blacks to sell the precious land they had acquired from the state, and by 1936 there were only 300 blacks left on Daufuskie. There had been 3,000 only 70 years before. Savannah factories began dumping chemical wastes in the waters around the two islands, and the pollution killed the fishing industry. Hunting, however, remained good enough to allow some few blacks – and even fewer whites – to survive.

Often, island blacks made trips to Savannah in tiny sailboats to sell their produce and meat.

Mid-wifery was the only form of giving birth; consequently there were many stillbirths. Most of the inhabitants, especially men, died of strokes and heart attacks.

Changing times and plans offered attractive prices for land, and by 1940 the Hilton Head Company (later known as the Sea Pines Plantation Company and Association) began development on Hilton Head Island. Reachable only by boat as late as 1953, the island began a ferry service for cars and people, and soon stately homes appeared.

A public health center was opened, followed by a post office, and an electrical power plant. Sketches for a new bridge to the mainland were drawn, and by 1956 the James F. Burns Crossing was completed. Now anything was possible. Where Braddock Point fronted Calibogue Sound across from Daufuskie in 1861, now

218

stood Sea Pines Plantation and ultramodern Harbortown – probably the most affluent resort in all the Sea Islands. The wealthy from America and abroad come to spend their vacations playing tennis, golf, riding and swimming. Glamorous and luxurious, Harbortown is tucked in between a few old black cemeteries and moss-laden cypress trees.

But the 5000-acre island called Daufuskie does NOT experience the American dream. She does not touch the mainland by bridges or tunnels; boats remain the only mode of physical contact. Few Daufuskians wear watches and hardly know what day it is. They are the last bit of evidence of what the Sea Islands once represented; living proof of what was known as Low Country culture. Her people were close-knit, and gave her a reknown complex personality. No Cubans or Latins, Haitians, very few whites, and fewer newcomers who mainly came to teach school. The Daufuskians are like great chefs who keep those great recipes to themselves.

Over a three-and-a-half-year period, I spent a number of weeks on Daufuskie; usually from five to seven days at a time. My intention was to document her people. I found that those recipes were told in their faces. It took at least two years to make friends and to establish their trust. There had been many exaggerations and tall tales told about her.

No accurate photographic record had existed of Daufuskie. Ten years from now she will be another Sea Pines Plantation. Hilton Head natives deeply regret not having a pictorial record of their island 40 years ago. They helped me convince the Daufuskians to open their hearts and allow me to document her purity. Daufuskie wanted very much to be remembered as a survivor but now she fears for her life.

With the purchase of 2500 of Daufuskie's 5000 acres, land developers have brought major changes. It now plays host to a resort, Melrose Plantation, which is very successful and popular. While native Daufuskians welcome even the menial jobs made available, they are personally devastated by the changes in their Low Country, ancestral way of life. Yet they accept that it was probably inevitable."

Jeanne Moutoussamy-Ashe

THE ELBOW ROOM is proud to present DAUFUSKIE ISLAND, a stunning meditation on place by the New York based photographer Jeanne Moutoussamy-Ashe. Best known in Britain as the author of Viewfinders: Black Women Photographers 1839-1985, this is the first exhibition of her work in Britain. The exhibition is available for hire from The Elbow Room, P.O. Box 2, Hebden Bridge, West Yorkshire HX7.

LUBAINA HIMID, "Mirror Cloth Bowl", 1986

Lubaina Himid and Maud Sulter

Lubaina Himid and **Maud Sulter** are co-curatorial directors of The Elbow Room. As an independent space it stages challenging, exciting exhibitions internationally. As curators they are particularly passionate about Blackwomen's Creativity.

However as artists they have been exhibiting their work together in joint shows since 1987.

A Room for MaShulan, Rochdale Art Gallery (1987), *Blackwomansong*, Sisterwrite, London (1988), *Gold Blooded Warrior*, Tom Allen Centre, London (1988), *Treatise on the Sublime*, University Art Gallery, California, State University, Stanislaus (1990).

In addition **Maud Sulter** has produced audio and video tapes to accompany Lubaina Himid's solo shows: *A Fashionable Marriage*, Pentonville Gallery, London (1986), and *The Ballad of the Wing*, Chisenhale Gallery, London (1989). They entered a joint piece in *Along the Lines of Resistance*, Cooper Gallery, Barnsley (1988).

The making of the installation *A Room for Mashulan* was difficult, painful, unpredictable and frightening. What was needed was trust, understanding, support and democracy. We achieved bits of these some of the time. We tried not to compromise. We tried to share things; skills, resources, materials, space and experience. We succeeded some of the time.

LUBAINA: "I wanted to continue what I had started with *mirror/cloth/bowl* and try to find the points at which my grandmother and I became/become one woman. The pieces I have made are the method I am using to speak to her. I want her to speak to me and give me the strength to go home and to have home within me."

MAUD: "For me the energy in and of the room is equal to the energy

we virtually bled into it. Working with other Blackwomen artists was not new to either of us but here we tore down with our bared souls barriers so often imposed/unchallenged in the past. Differences were challenged; privilege, likes, dislikes, beliefs, fears, hopes, aspirations."

The spirit of MaShulan is with us still and should we ever be apart she will always be with each of us. As grandmother. As forebearer. As sister. As woman. As one.

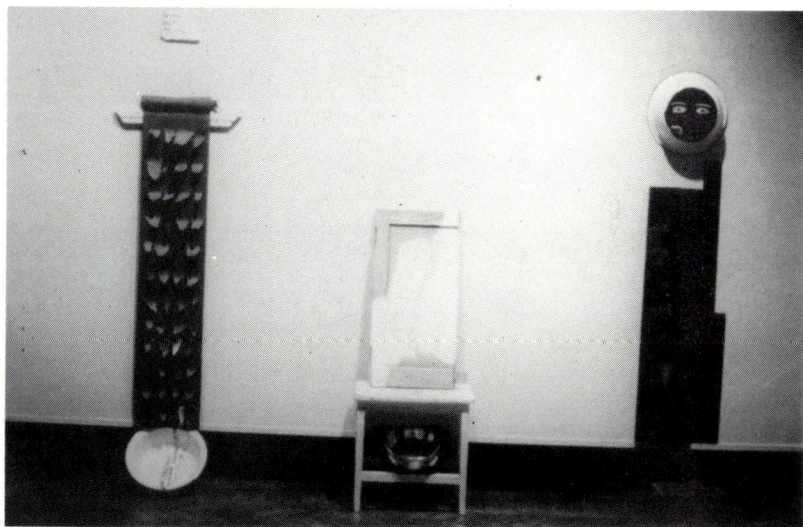

Lubaina Himid, "Mirror Cloth Bowl", *A Room for MaShulan*, 1986

Lubaina Himid, "Wing Woman"; *Gold Blooded Warrior*, 1988

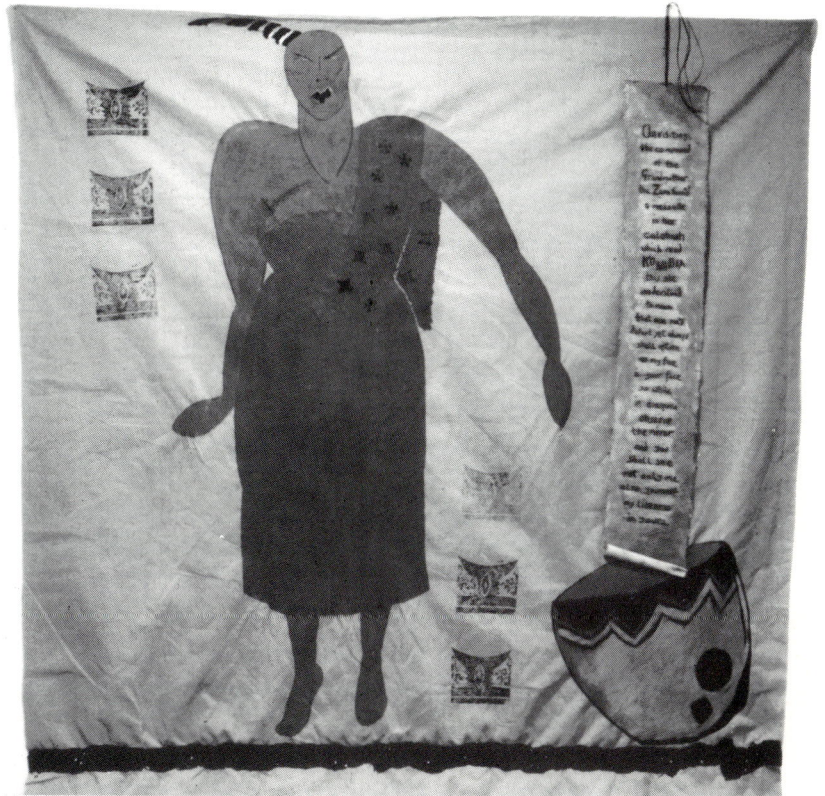

Maud Sulter, "The Message" *Gold Blooded Warrior*, 1988

"Zenobia traces the rich and varied adventures of Blackwomen in Europe from 245BC to 1954, from Hannibal's sister crossing the Alps to the artist arriving in Blackpool, UK. In each work a moment in history is coupled with an object/ symbol which transcends that moment and is passed on to us through time."

Lubaina Himid, 1990

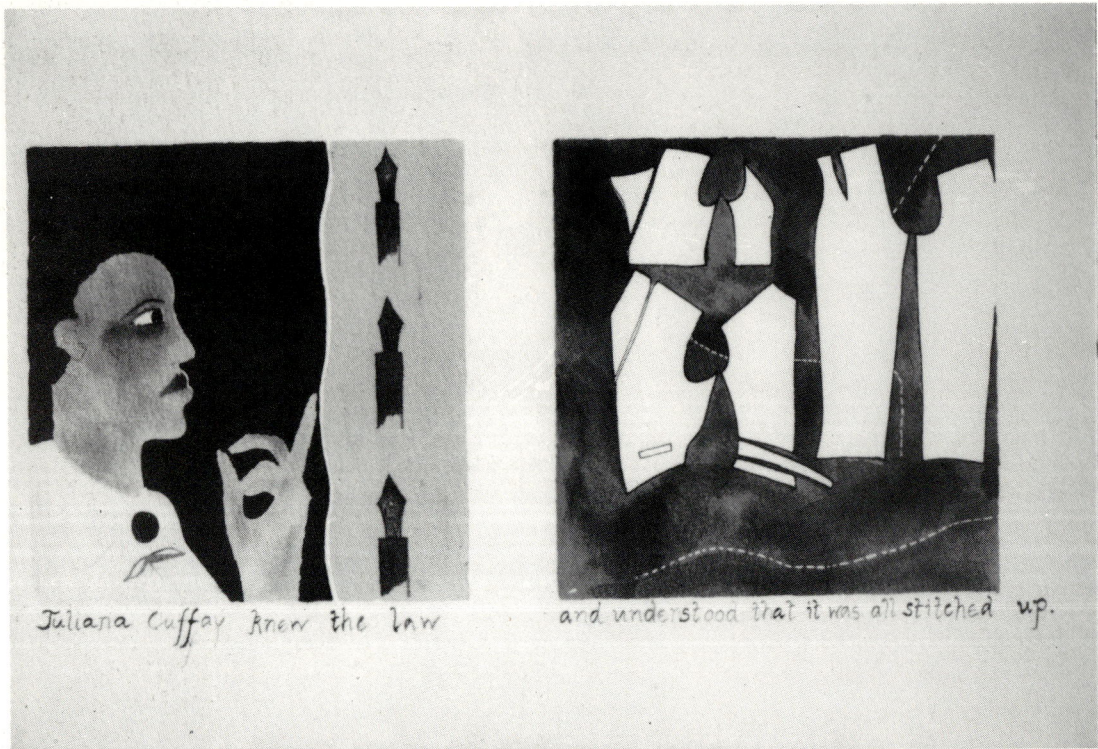

Lubaina Himid, "Zenobia", *Treatise on the Sublime*, 1990

Maud Sulter, "Paris Noir', *Treatise on the Sublime*, 1990.

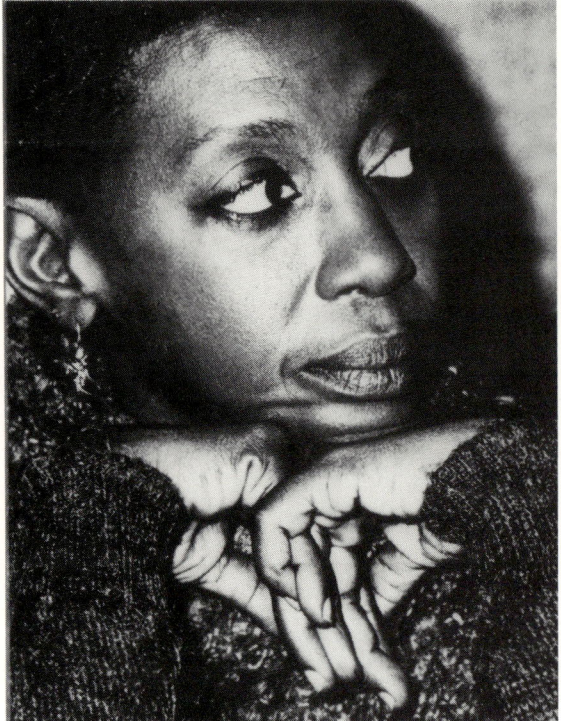

TESTIMONY: Three Blackwomen photographers, poster 1986

Section Four **TESTIMONY**

This section is a short introduction to the range of activities the Black-women's Creativity Project has been involved in since 1982 both as an autonomous organisation and in collaboration with The Elbow Room, FAN and WedG. It does not seek to be comprehensive or chronological but simply lets you glimpse our archive which includes independent curatorial work by Lubaina Himid.

GALLERY 5 BLACK WOMEN·AFRICA CENTRE

Paintings, Drawings and Sculpture
by
Sonia Boyce
Lubaina R A Himid
Claudette Johnson
Houria Niati
Veronica Ryan

Africa Centre Gallery,
38 King Street, London WC2.
September 6th to October 14th
Monday to Friday 10.00 to 5.30.
You are invited to a private view
Tuesday September 6th, 6.30-8.30

THE THIN BLACK LINE

BRENDA AGARD · SUTAPA BISWAS · SONIA BOYCE · CHILA BURMAN · JENNIFER COMRIE
LUBAINA HIMID · CLAUDETTE JOHNSON · INGRID POLLARD · VERONICA RYAN
MAUD SULTER · MARLEN SMITH

CONCOURSE GALLERY and UPPER STAIRCASE 15 NOVEMBER 1985 – 26 JANUARY 1986   AN EXHIBITION SELECTED BY LUBAINA HIMID
UPPER GALLERY 15 NOVEMBER – 30 NOVEMBER 1985   STAIRCASE 15 NOVEMBER 1985 – 1 JUNE 1986

ICA THE MALL LONDON SW1 01-930 3647   OPENING VIEW THURSDAY 14 NOVEMBER 1985 6.00-9.00

top   5 BLACK WOMEN AT THE AFRICA CENTRE
           Invite 1983
bottom   THE THIN BLACK LINE
           Invite 1985

230

Africa Centre 38 King Street London WC2E 8JT 01-836 1973

PRESS RELEASE (for immediate use)

5 Black Women: Exhibition of Drawings, Paintings and Sculpture

In the Africa Centre Gallery from 5 September to 14 October there
will be an exhibition of work by five young black women currently
living in Britain.

The artists have chosen to exhibit together although the work of
each is highly individual and makes its own artistic and political
statement. As the first major show by women to be mounted in the
Africa Centre Gallery the exhibition will demonstrate, both
collectively and individually, some of the experiences and concerns
of black women whose observations and critique are expressed
through art.

Two of the artists are African, two British-born of West Indian
parentage and one was born in the Caribbean and educated in
Britain.

Houria Niati, from Algeria, creates a multi-coloured and intricate
"background painting" of dreams and free-flowing images, to which
she fixes objects and instruments suggesting barriers, repression
and torture.

Lubaina Himid, from Tanzania, draws startling and funny visual
images ("though men don't often find them funny") to challenge the
sexual and political power of men who are racists and misogynists.

Claudette Johnson paints in dark, rich colours. Her subjects are
women: women finding their strength, women in struggle.

Sonia Boyce's large pastel drawings are her wry perceptions and
memories of familiar domestic scenes, evoked through larger-than-
life close-up views of small details: the back of a woman's head,
a child's dancing feet, the swollen legs and feet of a working
woman.

Veronica Ryan creates small intimate sculptures which have the
appearance of objects found on a beach or in a forest clearing,
formed 2000 years ago or made yesterday.

During the exhibition there will be an accompanying programme of
evening events: discussions with the artists (using slides)
about the form and motivation of their work; a performance by
Houria Niati to complement her work through song and words; and a
dialogue between women writers and women visual artists about their
varying and mutual concerns and aspirations.

P.T.O

DIRECTOR GENERAL Dr ALASTAIR NIVEN MA Ph D
Reg. Charity No. 313510

5 BLACK WOMEN AT THE AFRICA CENTRE
Press Release 1983

The Elbow Room

PASSION is a provocative theme for the first International exhibition of contemporary Blackwomens creativity of the African diaspora. Not because it enters the dangerous terrain of pleasure and danger. No, its provocation lies in the authority of these artists to engage on their own terms in the creation of art around an area blanketed in a patriarchal necrophiliac shroud.

BEAUTY has been denied us; as a potential, as a reality, as a self-definition. The legacy of slaveocracy shackles us still. Crude misrepresentations of our sexuality still try to coerce Blackwomen into subservient roles. However the depth and quality of the works commissioned for PASSION bears testimony to the value of trust between the artists. In understanding the power of the domestic interior and the translation of work from private to public each woman confronts her own PASSIONS.

The personal passion of the Blackwoman warrior is evoked in the b & w photography of **Angele Etoundi Essamba.** Born in Carmeroon, now based in Amsterdam and well exhibited both there and in Paris, this is the first showing of her work in Britain. **Lubaina Himid's** passionate portrait bursts forth from the canvas creating a frisson of repressed energy in muted shades. Born in Zanzibar she came to England as a baby. **Ingrid Pollard** was four when she arrived in London from Guyana. Best known as a photographer she presents here a filmic letter from New York. Brixton based Blackamerican **Rita Keegan** continues her exploration of portraits and the family album. An early exponent of copyart she can manipulate the medium beyond rhetoric into the heady realm of art and beauty. **Dionne Sparks,** premiered here in her first Blackwomens show, uses fabric and found objects to create messages across time and space. A native daughter of Washington D.C. **Michelle Parkerson's** films STORME and GOTTA MAKE THIS JOURNEY (featuring Sweet Honey in the Rock) will be on continuous video showing throughout the run of the show creating a counterpoint to the newly commissioned work of the other five artists.

SEX is not seen as a mere physical act which can be seperated from the social and economic environments of the diaspora. Although there is a tremendous pressure on Blackwomens creativity to cease to exist as a liberating practice it is still possible to counter the hegemonic, nihilistic and infact life threatening behaviour which persists in encouraging pornography in place of eroticism, rape in place of relationships and breeding in place of mothering. Each artist in this exhibition has engaged with these realities. Which is why it privileges above all else the political passion of Blackwomens relationships with each other; as sisters, as lovers, as friends.

LUST in the guise of a genuine on going need is paramount in the continuity of not only the staging of Blackwomens exhibitions but also the more individual and often private process of the production of the work. This exhibition is one of a continuum. 5 BLACK WOMEN AT THE AFRICA CENTRE, BLACK WOMEN TIME NOW, THE THIN BLACK LINE, TESTIMONY, are sister exhibitions to PASSION. Without each ground breaking step no Blackwoman would have **both** recognition **and** the opportunity to name herself in the myriad facets of her being, **Black Woman Artist.**

LOVE is much maligned in this society. So let us stand back and contemplate these PASSIONS. A complex calyx of beauty, pleasure and desire rooted firmly in Pan africanist herstories. The message is clear,

'We will be who we want to be.

        The time is now and the word is freedom.'

ENJOY!

MAUD SULTER
March 1989

PASSION: Blackwomen's Creativity of the African Diaspora
Statement 1989

PASSION: Blackwomen's Creativity of the African Diaspora
Poster 1989

BLACKWOMEN WRITERS

GEN DOUBLE ISSUE LITERARY SUPPLEMENT

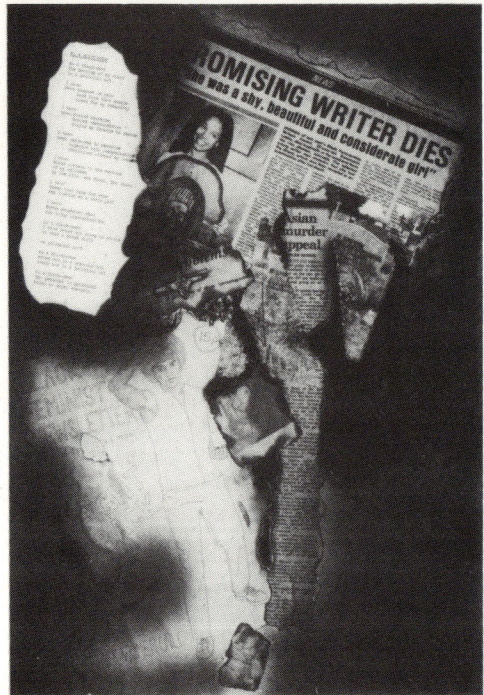

FICTION   SET UP A WRITING GROUP   POETRY

GEN: Blackwomen Writers Supplement
Cover 1986

GEN: Supplement
Pull out poster 1986

REVIEWS

BETSEY BROWN by Ntozake Shange
Methuen Press

Betsey's story flows like the easy rhythm of a familiar song. That song carried experiences held by so many through their adolescence. For Betsey, however, the rhythm is not even in tempo, but turbulent as the experiences of all blacks living in the southern states of America in the 1950s.

Betsey's political understanding and positive self and family images were very exciting. Throughout the book the strengths of black people are reflected in different ways the Jane, Greer, Carrie and Betsey herself.

Ntozake Shange dramatically portrays the excitement of the Civil Rights' movement on the Brown family with tremendous realism of the tokenistic laws and the anxiety of those desperate for their rights. She so vividly describes how the Browns are caught up in the fears of compulsory bussing and the doubts of its aims. The bitter sweet distress of the children adds momentum to the reader's anxiety. To be enjoyed by all ages and should be seen as a refreshing source of stimulation to English texts when reading of those times in America.

Jacqui Verrall

LAND OF ROPE AND TORY
by Marsha PRESCOD
Akira Press Poetry Series, available from
PO Box 409, London E2 7EU

Marsha Prescod has been living and working in England since the 1950's. She was encouraged initially by the Black Writers Workshop in Brixton and has been writing poetry since 1980. Brent Black Music Workshop helped her to develop her own style and confidence as a 'performance poet'. *Land of Rope and Tory* is a collection of several years work she has performed around the country. She writes firstly for Blackpeople, using our humour to win over those of us whose only (alienating) experience of poetry was perhaps, at school.

She covers a range of experience and politics in her work, commenting on the lives and concerns of Blackpeople in struggle. All of her work is powerful and thought-provoking, it catches up your thoughts, and left me nodding my head in recognition. The ones that moved me particularly

16

include 'Death by Self-Neglect', which is Marsha's favourite — and her personal preference for the title of this collective. She describes this as the '. . . second and best poem I ever wrote. . .' The title is taken from the coroner's verdict of the death of Richard Campbell's while in police custody. Through her poem she draws out some of the universality of our experience, letting '. . . a group of bigshot whitemen talking. . .' from Uruguay, America, 'Sout' Africa' and 'great britain' do the rest.

In 'Warrior Woman's song' I felt she touched on the economic, sexual and cultural abuse of our peoples and our land, reminding us of what can be and is Blackwomen's unique contribution to the survival of our peoples. 'They're Playing Our Song' reminds us of the 'slavery' of capitalism, and how it is reflected in our lives today. I liked 'Old Timers' for not letting us religate our elders to a 'dead' past, reminding us of their struggles — uprisings and 'riots' didn't happen only now, within our generation 'in Brixton'! 'Love Story' (parts one and two) carry on our womanist traditions of commenting, to good effect, on our relationships and experiences with Blackmen.

I liked all of Marsha's work, my enjoyment reinforced by having also seen her in performance in the past. Blackwomen have herstorically used humour, as a tool of survival, to deal with horrors of our loss, and to pass on our skills and strategies. Marsha's work is about us recognising the racism around us, and the need to tell and re-define our experiences in our own words which she sums up in this 'Untitled' piece:

```
UNTITLED
FOR US TO BE FREE
WE HAVE TO KNOW WE
DON'T LET ANYONE 'ETHNICIZE' US,
INTO THEM MARGINAL CATEGORIES.

OUR POSITIVE SELF CANNOT BE,
THROUGH NEGATIVE DEFINITION,
SAYING, 'WELL, WE'RE NOT THEM'
TO WORK OUT OWN POSITION.

DON'T LOOK TO HIS STORY
TO DISCOVER OUR EXISTENCE
DON'T HIDE IN ANOTHER'S IDEASOLOGY
TO DEVELOP OUR OWN RESISTANCE
                              BLACK
FOR US TO BE FREE,          BLACK
WE HAVE TO KNOW WE.         BLACK
OUR OWN TRUTH               BLACK
OUR OWN STRENGTH,
AND OUR              CREATIVITY!
```

If you feel urged to action, perhaps you'll take Marsha's advice and go out and order our books for libraries and '. . . institutionalize our presence. . .', so that in twenty years time we'll not be invisible to our children, as the Black Communities of 20-30 years ago appear to be to us. And give our children some of the humour that is and has been a strong part of our survival.

* * * * * * * * * * * * * * * * * * * *

Dorothea Smartt, November 1985

Betsey Brown, A novel by Ntozake Shange,
reviewed by Jacqui Verrall
Land of Rope and Tory, Poetry by Marsha Prescod
Reviewed by Dorothea Smartt
GEN: Blackwomen Writers Supplement

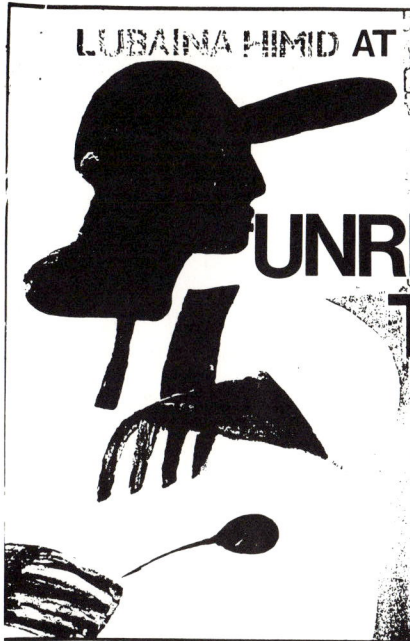

LUBAINA HIMID AT **THE ELBOW ROOM** presents

UNRECORDED TRUTHS

APRIL 16 MAY 16

MON–SAT 10–5

**BRENDA AGARD
SIMONE ALEXANDER
DAVID BAILEY
SUTAPA BISWAS
SONIA   BOYCE
ALLAN deSOUZA
KEITH PIPER
DONALD RODNEY
MARLENE SMITH**

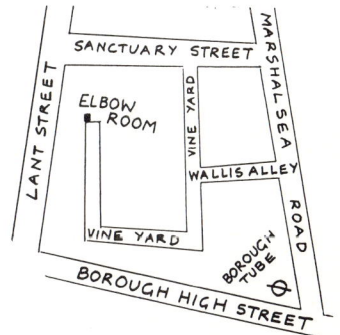

SANCTUARY STREET
LANT STREET
ELBOW ROOM
VINE YARD
MARSHALSEA ROAD
WALLIS ALLEY
VINE YARD
BOROUGH TUBE
BOROUGH HIGH STREET

the elbow room is in VINE YARD SEI

UNRECORDED TRUTHS
Catalogue cover 1986

237

I made this piece for us.
I am trying to make an image of a
Black woman.
Do you know her ?
This image is not about faces, eyes, lips,
breasts, thighs, hips......................
This is an image about living a life.
Do you know it ?

As a child I dusted flowers like the ones in
this piece. Then I hated them.
Today, placing them in this context
I am using them as a vehicle
around which I make images of
ourselves and our struggle.
The hatred is vanquished.
The understanding

is developing

I made this image
of a Black woman for us.
Do you know her ?

UNRECORDED TRUTHS
Catalogue statement, MARLENE SMITH

BLACKWOMANSONG

BLACKWOMANSONG
NEW WORKS ON PAPER
MAUD SULTER & LUBAINA HIMID
at SISTERWRITE GALLERY
190 UPPER STREET, LONDON N1
For times call 01-226-9782

FRIDAY 9th DECEMBER UNTIL
SATURDAY 7th JANUARY 1989

Waiting for the bus, by Lubaina Himid

You are invited to the women only launch of
BLACKWOMANSONG
At Sisterwrite Gallery, 190 Upper Street
7 - 9p.m. on Thursday 8th December
▼ Refreshments courtesy The Elbow Room

Phoenix come rise
from the flame
through gold light
to orange fire
sparked smoke
darting wayward

Reclaiming
that which was
ours which is now
ours again

Unknown words
dance like
mirambas
across
the space
and time
between us

We become one

From **SPHINX** by Maud Sulter

BLACKWOMANSONG
Invite 1989

SPHINX^x, poster

EXCLUSIVE PREVIEW: DAUFUSKIE ISLAND

LUBAINA HIMID AND MAUD SULTER GUEST EDIT...PASSION-

BLACKWOMEN'S CREATIVITY OF THE AFRICAN DIASPORA

with theory, painting, poetry, photography, prose and lots, lots more...

FAN Vol. 2 No. 8
Cover 1988

Opera in Africa is a sorrowful song

Dress and the observation of ritual

OMOYIOLA OYELEYE

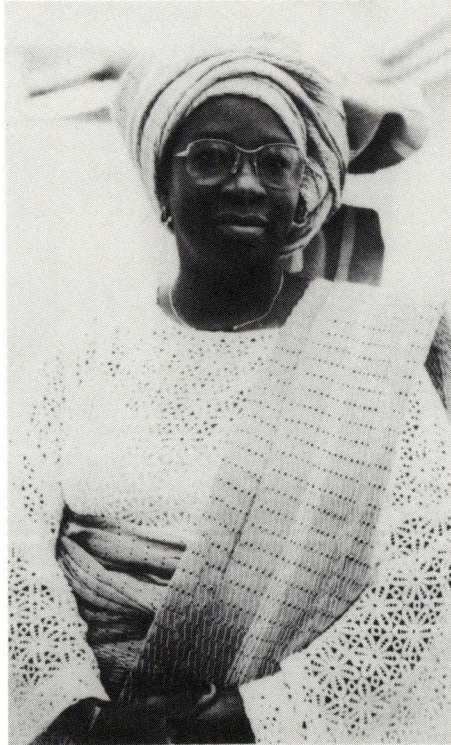

There are three important times or occasions in a human life. The two carry the feelings of happiness in births and weddings, the sad one is death and each one has their traditional dress.

In the olden days in Nigeria, the part of the world where I was born, when a child is born whether male or female, his name or hers remains secret until the eighth day. He or she would be called 'ikoko', 'Alejo', 'omo', 'Titun'. The meaning of all these names is 'a new arrival'. On the eighth day the child would be named. It is a big ceremony with feasting, dancing and if the child is a boy, it is followed by circumcision. Nowadays the traditions are dying off, you can know the sex of the child you are having and even name him or her before birth.

Wedding is also a big ceremony, which starts from the day of the engagement. The groom gives his wife presents and pays a dowry. This could be in money or ornaments - gold, valuable stones and nowadays with a bible. The wedding follows and the celebrants have a 'uniform' of handwoven cloth which has white and silver thread woven through it to denote a special occasion. This is called 'aso oke'. The newly-weds wear the traditional dress made from the woven material. The celebrants will also buy in bulk a particular design, which their guests will buy from them and sew. The style, however, is up to each person's taste. The 'aso oke' is generally worn by the adults, as it tends to be too heavy for children. The bride will also wear gold and coral beads.

The wedding is performed during the day, but the bride is always escorted to the bridegroom's house in the evening. She is then received by the senior wife of the bridegroom's family.

Death, which is always the end of everything, is very expensive. The children of the dead wear 'sanyan'. As for caring for the mourners, traditionally there are some people who rejoice in shedding crocodile tears and they would stay at the ceremony for days eating and drinking - some of the mourners might not even know the dead. They are 'professional mourners'. It is not easy to drive them away. In case they are ignored they quickly ask for their food and drinks.

Opera in Africa is a sorrowful song, a song that would make the children of the dead cry because it would have been composed for that particular dead person. Both men and women sing and the best singer gets the attention and money from the children of the dead. There is no conductor and mostly the opera 'rara' lasts seventeen days. Then comes the memorial service every year according to the children's abilities.

Nowadays only a few people pay attention to the traditions.

Omoyiola Oyeleye

FAN Vol. 2 No. 8
Article by Mrs. Oyeleye

The second stage of the GOLD BLOODED WARRIOR Exhibition and part of the TOWARDS TOMORROW FESTIVAL of Blackwoman's Art and Performance, co-ordinated by Brenda Agard.

Artists exhibited were Abiola Agana, Carol Maloney, Frederica Brooks, Janette Parris, Jeanette Davis, Ladan Nourbakhsh, Marcia Thomas, Marilyn Hawthorne, Sandra Grant and Stella Lymas.

BLACKWOMANPRINTPROJECT: May 19th - June 10th 1988

Feeling a bit jaded as old timers in the field of Blackwomen's Creativity, we staged THE GOLD BLOODED WARRIOR with the express aim of making fresh contacts with other Blackwomen working in the field of image/text production. Much to our pleasure and delight we have now met and skill-shared with many new and exciting Blackwomen artists.

The experimental Print Workshops incorporated: discussions of the politics of being Blackwomen artists, exhibiting, and technical know-how – while working in a positive environment.

The work on show was selected from the many pieces produced over the three days, and all of the women who took the plunge, and had some 'hands on' experience, have at least one piece exhibited.

Using simple methods of expression, for the illustration of the many complicated nuances; the pleasures, the pain, the passion of Blackwomen's experience, allows us to broaden our visual awareness.

Although many of the women have not exhibited before, this vibrant and challenging work moves us all.

TOWARDS TOMORROW   Maud Sulter & Lubaina Himid

ABIOLA AGANA
Some people watch life
Some people laugh
Others cry,
Some don't get a chance,
Catch up with life ...
Before it catches up with you.
        Abiola Agana (14 years)

CAROL MALONEY
My name is Carol Maloney –
I've studied design for the last three years
– this is the first day I've felt enthusiastic for ages!

FREDERICA BROOKS
I am a Blackwoman artist living in London.
I know that the use of text in my work will mean something to many who feel the importance of letters for keeping essential ties with family and loved ones when apart.

JANETTE PARRIS
My name is Janette Parris.
I came
I took part
I was educated.

JEANETTE DAVIS
My name is Jeanette Davis.
My participation in the Blackwomens Workshop has been an educating and stimulating experience because it has made me question my existence as a Black Artist.

LADAN NOURBAKHSH
Studying at Sheffield City Polytechnic – Fine Art.
Spending this time working with little materials, space or time has been a great experience – just because it's so good to be with other black women making something new.
Haven't had such a good time in ages.

MARCIA THOMAS
Life for life
Eye for eye
Tooth for tooth...
Wound for wound
Opportunity may be long coming –
Don't wait for it
Go for it!
I'm Marcia Thomas, AND I TRY

MARILYN HAWTHORNE
I work full time (out of art) and I am interested in all kinds of Black Art, especially sculpture.

SANDRA GRANT
My name is Sandra Grant, and I am a 2nd year Graphic Design student at East Ham Community College.
The work I produced, I feel, has come out better than I expected. I was confident to approach the subject matter and felt quite relaxed in the Workshop's friendly atmosphere. I thoroughly enjoyed myself.

STELLA LYMAS
Art as an Expression
of life itself.
Art as an expression
of feeling, questioning, and challenging
the world we live in, and assumptions
that try to repress me,
Women,
Blacks,
Humanity.

TEXTS CITED

BLACK SISTER: Poetry by Black American Women, 1746-1980
Ed. Erlene Stefson
Pub. Indiana University Press

HEART OF THE RACE
Ed. Dadzie, Bryan, Scafe
Pub. Virago

THE HIDDEN FACE OF EVE
Nawal El Saadawi
Pub. Zed Press

THE POETRY OF THE NEGRO
Ed. Hughes & Bontemps
Pub. Doubleday

POEMS OF BLACK AFRICA
Ed. Wole Soyinka

AS A BLACKWOMAN
Maud Sulter
Pub. Urban Fox Press

OUT THERE FIGHTING

ABIOLA	AGANA
CAROL	CROSBY
CHILA	KUMARI BURMAN
CLAUDETTE	JOHNSON
DAVE	LEWIS
DAVID	A. BAILEY
DIONNE	SPARKS
DONALD	RODNEY
EDDIE	CHAMBERS
FRANKLYN	BECKFORD
FREDERICA	BROOKS
INGRID	POLLARD
JANETTE	PARRIS
JENNY	McKENZIE
JOSEPH	MENDY
KEITH	PIPER
LADAN	NOURBAKHSH
LUBAINA	HIMID
MARCIA	THOMAS
MAUD	SULTER
NINA	EDGE
PITIKA	NTULI
POGUS	CAESAR
RASHEED	ARAEEN
RITA	KEEGAN
RHONA	HARRIETTE
SALEEM	ARIF
SAMENA	RANA
TAM	JOSEPH
TONY	WILLIAMS
VERONICA	RYAN
WINSTON	JAMES
ZARINA	BHIMJI

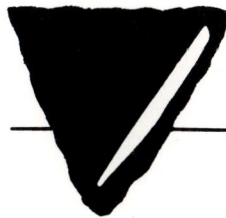

an elbow room show

OUT THERE FIGHTING
Invite 1988

245

A FASHIONABLE MARRIAGE
Poster 1986

NEW ROBES FOR MaSHULAN

LUBAINA HIMID WORK PAST & PRESENT

A ROOM FOR MaSHULAN
MAUD SULTER & LUBAINA HIMID

NEW ROBES FOR MaSHULAN
Poster 1987

GOLD BLOODED WARRIOR
Poster 1988

Empowerment

There is no simple conclusion to a book such as this. Because it attempts to record a series of events and publications which have contributed to the history of the Blackwomens Creativity Project since 1982 it is informed by the situation in which the Project has functioned over that period. Alice Walker has noted that as Black women we read history for clues not facts. This collection does not seek to be exhaustive. It merely seeks to posit clues for those who may take up the challenge of further documenting this period (and other periods) of our production.

The priority for all forward thinking people should be to prioritise access for Blackwomen to this information. While we recognise that the information contained in this book is invaluable to all people, black and white, male and female, which is why it is a vital text for schools and higher education courses as well as general libraries and community venues, it is essential that Blackwomen are given access to the text. It is also vital that they are allowed the space to construct a critique.

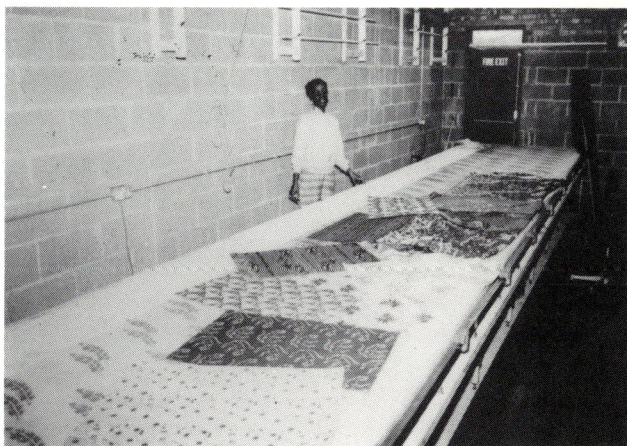

LESLEE WILLS, textile designer

It seems expedient to suggest that where white folks wish to engage in the debate that their first line of enquiry, having given adequate intellectual engagement to the text and images, may be into the nature of racism within the Artsand the rest of Society and how white people can help stamp it out - starting with themselves.

Good places to look for further clues include publications such as Artrage, Bazaar, FAN, Outwrite, Spare Rib, Time Out, City Limits, WASL journal, Ten.8 and We Are Here.

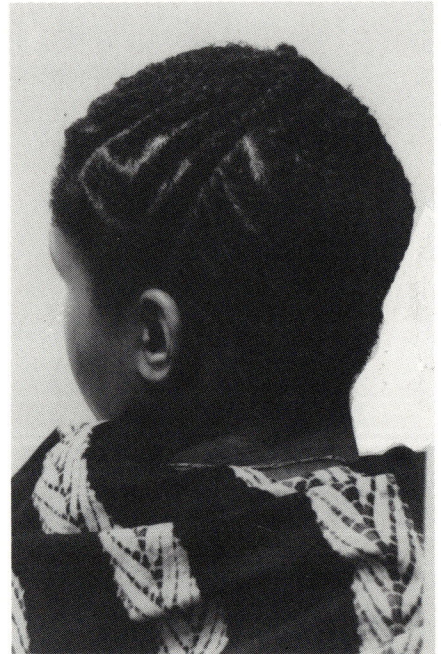

HAIRBRAIDING

Blackwomen have occasionally been allowed to write on cultural production in other publications but across the board there has seldom been the opportunity to develop skills consistently over a period of time. One notable exception was Akua Rugg, a selection of whose writings from Race Today Review was published under the title of Brickbats and Bouquets.

This cultural vacuum has led to a crisis in both the art of constructive criticism and the ability of the artist or writer to accept that criticism and take on board the issues which would arise from such a practice. If our creativity is to continue to grow then it must be open to such critiques and must indeed be subjected to the same.

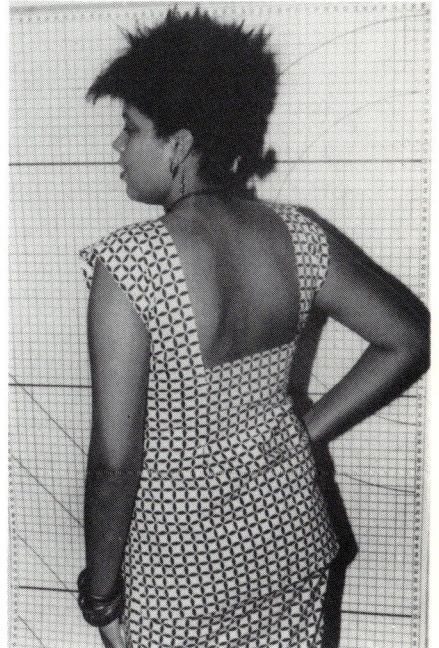

THERESA, modelling her own designs

When we look back over the past decade we see that against the odds we have managed to continue to move forward as various collective groupings and movements. However it would be wrong to become complacent in our victories.

With the rise in sexism, racism and fascism in the 'new" europe and it seems across the globe, we have a resonsibility to confront this spectre with our creativity. However we must not forget that our primary audience should be ourselves. As without positive sustenance we cannot fight a foe which is already planted within the societies in which we find ourselves.

MEERA SYAL, "One of Us"

Blackwomens creativity is borne out of our spiritualities. It must not be sacrificied in the name of some greater good which refuses to acknowledge our strengths, sexualities and gender, all of which are informed by our Blackness creating a wholeness with which to confront and create the world as we find it and the world we would like to inhabit.

SUSAN, at work

Blackwomen's Creativity is larger than any one individual and global in its potential.   We shall take care of our blessings.

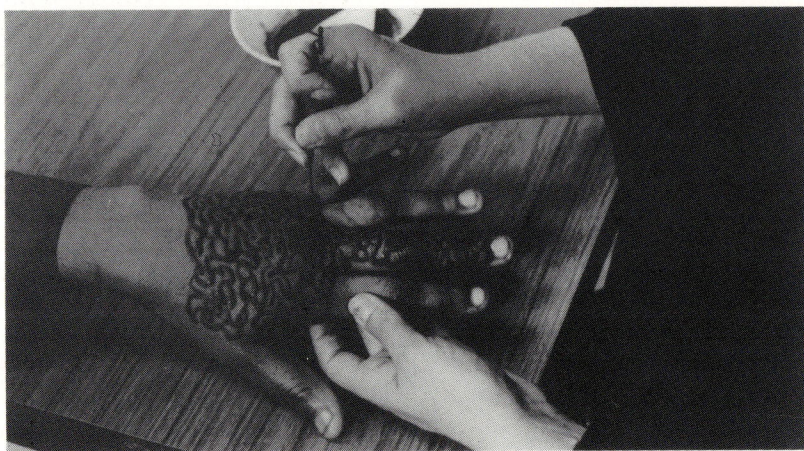

BODY HENNAING

URBAN FOX PRESS

OTHER TITLES IN THIS SERIES INCLUDE:

| THE THIN BLACK LINE | *"A sublime act of cultural terrorism."*

Eleven black women artists, including Sonia Boyce, Sutapa Biswas, Brenda Agard, Chila Burman and Veronica Ryan, exhibited at the ICA in 1985. This is their analysis of the whys and wherefores of their art. Accompanied by eleven installation shots of the works exhibited and a challenging comment by Lubaina Himid, the show's curator, outlining an uncompromising strategy for the nineties. A must for all art schools, artists and cultural historians.

Art/12pp/11B & W photos
Paperback £5.00
1-87 2124 0101

| DONALD RODNEY: CRITICAL |

A former member of the controverisal BLAK Art Group, Donald Rodney confronts the politics of the body, the urban milieu and international struggles un-compromisingly but with utter belief in victory over the powers of evil.

For the first time we have a publication which not only situates this fine young artist's work, but also allows him the opportunity, in words and pictures, to express his own hopes, fears and aspirations.

Art/12pp/B&W
Paperback £5.00
1-872124 216

| CLAUDETTE JOHNSON: PUSHING BACK THE BOUNDARIES |

The beauty of the work of Claudette Johnson does not eclipse the profoundly political nature of her work. Untainted by ambition or rhetoric it exists. It is profound.
"The Black women in my drawings are monoliths. Larger than life versions of women, invisible to white eyes, and naked to our own."

Art/12pp/B&W
Paperback £5.00
1-872124 267

URBAN FOX PRESS

PO Box 2, Hebden Bridge, W. Yorks HX7 6LW
TEL: (0422) 845504 FAX: (0422) 842590

URBAN FOX PRESS was established in 1989. Committed to publishing only the most exciting and dynamic works of fine art and literature. UFP is particularly passionate about Blackwomen's creatvity across continents.

HELP US CONTINUE to expand by ordering your books now. All pre-orders will be despatched on publication day. As a Press we receive no subsidy or sponsorship and rely on you, our readers, to:

- order direct – we pride ourselves on our speed;

- encourage bookshops, libraries and educational institutions to add our titles to their shelves;

- facilitate readings and talks by our authors and, of course

- pass on the word about just how exciting our list is – and promises to remain!

OUR 1991 LIST is full of energising poetry, fiction and art. FORTHCOMING titles will include yet more International fiction, poetry and cultural theory. BE SURE of keeping in touch with UFP – join our mailing list today.

TRADE DISTRIBUTION

BOOKSPEED
48 Hamilton Place, Edinburgh, EH3 5AX
Tel: 031 225 4950 FAX: 031 220 6515